To Know and Follow Jesus

Thomas N. Hart

To Know
and Follow Jesus

Contemporary Christology

PAULIST PRESS
New York/Ramsey

Library of Congress
Catalog Card Number: 84-80354

ISBN: 0-8091-2636-2

Published by Paulist Press
545 Island Road, Ramsey, N.J. 07446

Printed and bound in the
United States of America

Contents

Introduction

Those who love Christ Jesus have always desired to know him better. Having found salvation and inspiration for their lives in him, they have wanted to understand all they can about him—his life and teaching, his relationship to God, his inner experience, his death and resurrection, and the relevance all this has for human life. This never ending quest has prompted theologians of every age to keep researching and re-thinking the person of Jesus and everything that pertains to him. What makes Christians Christians is, after all, their belief in and love of Jesus Christ.

Christology is that part of theology which reflects on Jesus, and Christology is very much alive in the contemporary Church. Theologians are closely re-examining the New Testament, critically reviewing the great Christological councils, and reformulating our Christological faith in the light of contemporary knowledge and needs.

There are several reasons why theologians are particularly active in Christology today. Recent biblical scholarship has taught us to approach the New Testament with different glasses, to distinguish its historical layers, to be aware of its interpretive editing, and to acknowledge its many different Christologies. An emergent recognition of historicity is another key factor. We now realize that all understanding and utterance is culturally situated. When we study the pronouncements of Church councils past, we recognize that they speak within specific horizons of understanding, and are limited still further by the particular questions they are trying to address. Some of the questions being asked today are different, and the horizons of understanding are different. This too contributes to the impetus for reformulation.

Religious pluralism is another factor. Conditions of modern mobility and the free exchange of information have placed us in a situation where all possible interpretations of life, religious and non-religious, swirl around us continually. The variety of religions and non-religious humanisms makes us ask: What, if anything, is distinctive about Jesus of Nazareth and the religion which comes after him? Does Christianity still deserve our allegiance? The problems of our age are a fourth factor in stimulating Christological interest. Besides the perennial challenges of human existence there are two large-scale problems in the contemporary world which are particularly acute. One is the immense economic imbalance which leaves most of the world's people poor. The other is the impending threat of total destruction by nuclear war. In our search for resources to help us grapple with these problems, we ask: Is there anything in the teaching or example of Jesus, or in the community which bears his name, that can be of use to us in our present situation?

A great many voices contribute to the Christological synthesis presented in this book. On the Roman Catholic side, there are Piet Schoonenberg, Edward Schillebeeckx, Karl Rahner, and Hans Küng. The Protestant theologians Rudolph Bultmann, Paul Tillich, and Dietrich Bonhoeffer, and the Anglicans D.M. Baillie and John Knox are heard here too. From Latin America there are the liberation theologians Gustavo Gutierrez, Juan Luis Segundo, Leonardo Boff, and Jon Sobrino. The school of process thought is likewise represented, by Alfred North Whitehead, Norman Pittenger, John Cobb, Jr., and David Griffin, along with Pierre Teilhard de Chardin, working independently yet along similar lines. Roman Catholic Scripture scholars Joseph Fitzmyer and Raymond Brown also have an important place. Other theologians have made significant contributions to Christology too. The above are mentioned by name because they have been the principal influences on the Christology presented here.

That a synthesis of such a broad sample of theologians is possible at all is due to the fact that although they exhibit some variety among themselves, there are strong lines of convergence in their thinking. This we will attempt to show. Theirs is not the only model of Christology in the Church today, but it is a solid and fruitful one, commanding respect precisely because their names are associated with it. These are careful scholars and Christian pastors. Their Christology stands in continuity with the Christology of generations past, yet is fresh and distinctive, interesting and compelling.

This book is an attempt to make this contemporary Christology available to the Church at large. Most ordinary Christians are not going to read Rahner, Schillebeeckx, or Cobb. They are too difficult, and, for many, also too long. But their ideas are invaluable. My hope is that this book might bring those ideas more within the reach of the Christian community.

Christology books have tended to be of two kinds, heady or devotional. They are written at an abstract intellectual level for professional theologians, or they are written at the level of the heart to help the average believer relate to Jesus. This book attempts to combine the two objectives, to speak to both head and heart. It is a work of pastoral theology, endeavoring at once to answer the perennial Christological questions discussed by theologians and to speak to every Christian's concern for the life of faith. I adopt this orientation because I am convinced that our devotion to Jesus needs to be solidly grounded, but also that theology's task is not finished until theologians have shown the relevance of their conclusions for Christian living.

The synthesis here presented is my own. I can hardly claim originality where the ideas are concerned. I have received them from others. But the interpretation of those ideas, the language, and the selection and arrangement are mine. Where these are faulty, I must bear the responsibility. The viewpoint is Roman Catholic, but I have been deeply influenced by theologians of other Christian denominations as well.

It is not my intent to impose contemporary Christological thinking on anyone. I would rather like to encourage the greatest measure of freedom with respect to the ideas presented here. For some, the book will simply serve to acquaint them with what is going on in Christology today. They will disagree with it. Others will find here an articulation of their present faith and will feel confirmed by what they read. Still others will find the Christology set forth here different from what they now hold and also more adequate and attractive, and they will allow their thinking to be changed. All of these responses are quite acceptable. There is much pluralism in the Christology of Christians today. There was already in New Testament times.

The layout of the book is a little different from that of many books on Christology. It does not start with the philosophical question of Jesus' constitution, the way humanity and divinity combine in him. It starts rather where Christianity started, with the experience of salvation. It was only because his contemporaries found Jesus a bearer of extraordinary saving help that they asked the question about who he was and where he had come from. Next comes the meaning of discipleship, the concrete living of the Gospel, which is sometimes also called Christian spirituality. Discipleship is what follows from being saved, and is already a participation in salvation. Then comes the question of Jesus' constitution as the Council of Chalcedon defined it, because it is at this point that the question of his identity is properly posed, and Chalcedon gave it its clearest, most influential answer. This leads to some critical reflections on Chalcedon offered by contemporary theologians, which prepare the way for their reformulation of Christological understanding. After setting out the reformulation both in the abstract and in the concrete, we look at some of the questions that are most frequently asked about it. Then we examine contemporary interpretations of the resurrection and its significance for us. Next comes a chapter on the peculiar contributions of liberation theology to our thinking about Jesus today. The book closes with a chapter on Christianity among the religions of the world.

I. The Experience of Salvation

When I was a student in Berkeley, I used to watch the preachers on the campus of the University of California. One of them would typically take a stand in front of the student center, Bible in hand, and begin to shout to the passing throng that they were all sinners, and that they needed the salvation that comes from Jesus Christ. Most of the students would just keep walking. Possibly they did not care about their salvation. Possibly they did not think they were sinners. Others would stop and listen for a minute, then walk on. It was hard to say what their reaction was. Others would heckle the preacher: "Shut up! You're disturbing the peace." "You think we're sinners. You're worse. *You* go to hell, you old fool." "You're crazier than a loon!"

The preaching did not seem to be too effective. It occured to me that telling people they were sinners may not be the best way to begin. Noticing the movements on campus which were successful, I also reflected that people are drawn to what they think will meet some need they have, or enhance their life in some way. Many were drawn to yoga and meditation workshops, to various forms of therapy, and to political activities geared to improving the possibilities for human life. Perhaps the preaching on campus was not meeting any felt need.

New Testament preaching began on a rather different note. It promised people something that would make their lives happier.

> Jesus said: "If only you recognized God's gift, and who it
> is that is asking you for a drink, you would have asked him

instead, and he would have given you living water" (Jn 4:10).

This is the good news about Jesus Christ, the Son of God (Mk 1:1).

Blessed be the God and Father of our Lord Jesus Christ, who in Christ has blessed us with every spiritual blessing in the heavenly realm (Eph 1:3).

We write to you about the Word of life, which has existed from the very beginning. We have heard it, we have seen it with our eyes; yes, we have seen it and our hands have touched it. When this life became visible, we saw it; so we speak of it and tell you about the eternal life which was with the Father and was made known to us (1 Jn 1:1–2).

They make it sound exciting, like something helpful, healing, and hopeful, that will speak to the trouble in which people find themselves. They recount the stories of a woman healed after years of hemorrhaging (Mk 6), of a man become sane and peaceful after years of crazy behavior in a graveyard (Mk 5), of a woman converted from a life of prostitution (Lk 7), of a tax collector who became an Apostle (Mt 9). They tell stories of a marvelous man named Jesus, who brought God near to them all, welcoming the discards of society and eating with them, while confronting the rich and powerful with a call to conversion. The Fourth Gospel tells it in symbols, describing Jesus and his impact by analogy with all manner of life-giving things: vine, good shepherd, water, bread, light, resurrection, wine, way, truth, life. John is trying to express what Jesus' followers have experienced in him: brand new life and the transformation of their communities. It is wonderful, and because it is wonderful they want to share it with others. It is these helpful, hopeful, life-giving things that are meant when the New Testament speaks of "salvation." It is as if they are saying, "He saved our lives!"

Christology is the study of Christ. Soteriology is the study of salvation, an integral part of Christology, in many ways the most important part because soteriology tells us what difference the Christ event makes. The irony is that many books on Christology say little or nothing about soteriology, devoting all their energy instead to a discussion of the identity of Jesus. This is at variance with the New Testament, where most space is devoted to the teaching of Jesus and to the ways he helps or saves us. Jesus' relationship with God is constantly in focus, but it is not under analysis. Those who encountered Jesus felt something happening to them, an experience they expressed in various ways, but it always comes down to a being somehow saved. It was this primary experience that led them to ask the next logical question: "Who is this man anyway, that he has such an effect on us?" The experience of salvation precedes the inquiry into Jesus' identity. And so we treat it first.

"Salvation" means different things to different Christians. To some it means heaven, and being saved means getting into heaven. So it refers entirely to the next life. To others it is tied directly to Jesus' death for us. He died for our sins. That is, he took the punishment for our sins on himself and made satisfaction to God, and thus we are saved from bearing that punishment ourselves. In reality, the New Testament notion of salvation is broader than either of these views. If we talk exclusively of the next life, or of the forgiveness of sins, we overlook many important dimensions of the salvation Jesus offers us. We may miss the real concerns people feel today, and, like the Berkeley preachers, be dismissed as useless.

SAVED FROM WHAT?

What are the factors and experiences which make human
life laborious and painful, which make us question whether life
has meaning or value, which cause us to lose heart and sometimes even wish for death? What afflicts and oppresses us and
makes us long to be free?

Sickness and every kind of physical pain.
Broken relationships, broken community.
Poverty.
Oppression, injustice, the denial of basic rights.
Losses—valuable persons, valuable things.
Guilt about the bad things we have done.
Fears about the future.
Alienation and loneliness.
Personal hurts, and subsequent anger and resentment.
Addictions, compulsions, obsessions.
Boredom, meaninglessness.
The evil things we see happening all around us.
Death.

Probably other items could be added, but the list names a good
many of the things that afflict us and make life seem a dubious
blessing. As we look it over, we can probably see ways of con-
densing it. It contains many variations on the theme of human
sinfulness and the suffering that results to oneself and others
from that sinfulness. It all seems to come down to sin and suffering. There remains death though, which robs us of those
dear to us and eventually puts an end to ourselves as well. Perhaps every suffering is in some way a death—a diminishment,
a loss, a blockage from life. Then death is the more compre-
hensive term, embracing every form of suffering. So perhaps
we could say that our problems come down to two: sin and
death. At this point, we are very close to the way Paul himself

conceptualizes the human problem. Can Jesus, or anybody else, say or do anything helpful to us as we grapple with the many forms of sin and death that darken the face of the earth?

Amid the wreckage of precisely such a broken situation, Jesus of Nazareth moved about doing good. He did a lot of teaching, teaching which if heeded could heal broken relationships and broken community, reduce poverty, and remove oppression. It could create a rather different type of human community than we find in many places. But Jesus did more than just teach. He healed diseases, both physical and mental. He forgave sins, giving people like Magdalene, Peter, and the woman taken in adultery a new lease on life. He confronted the religious and political authorities of his day on their abuse of power and their hypocrisy. He befriended tax collectors, prostitutes, and sinners, and ate and drank with them. He raised people from death. And when out of jealousy and fear powerful people conspired to do away with him, he submitted to an unjust and painful death out of love for God and human beings, trusting in the one he called Father. God raised him from death and glorified him, and in this glorious risen state he continued to manifest himself to those who believed in him.

It did not end with this man's life and what he could do himself. Where his teaching, his example, and his spirit prevailed among people, i.e., where he himself continued to be present, a new type of human community was created. See if it does not sound like a community which has been saved from the darkness we spoke of.

> All those who believed continued together in close fellowship and shared their belongings with one another. They would sell their property and possessions, and distribute the money among all, according to what each one needed. Day after day they met as a group in the temple, breaking bread together in their homes, partaking of food with glad

and humble hearts, praising God and enjoying the good
will of all the people. And every day the Lord added to
their number those who were being saved (Acts 2:44–47).

Imagine what life in society, or even in the Church,
would be like if it were lived on these principles. The passage
is a portrait of salvation, experienced in a community of people
who love one another and share life together. They still face
sickness and death. They are still vulnerable to natural disas-
ters like flood and fire. But their solidarity with one another
and their hope in God make these things much more bearable
than before. They are persecuted by outside elements and
some are put to death. But death no longer frightens them. Jesus has told them there is life after death, and has come back
to them after his own death. So what others call death, they
now call sleep. The death they fear is not the death of the
body, but the death that comes to the human spirit through a
sinful and hopeless life. What has happened to these people
they call "salvation." What they mean by it is a total transformation of their lives. And it comes to them through the teaching and example, the death and resurrection, the ongoing
healing and strengthening presence of Jesus among them. In
these things they find the solutions to their problems, a program to dedicate their lives to, and a hope that transcends
even death.

THE DEATH/RESURRECTION OF JESUS
AS OUR SALVATION

So far we have seen that salvation has many dimensions to
it, and that it comes to us from many different aspects of Jesus'
ministry. Yet in many Christian presentations of the matter,

salvation is tied almost exclusively to the death/resurrection of Jesus. Paul, for instance, in his letters reiterates nothing of the teaching or miracles of Jesus; he writes only of Jesus' death/resurrection and their saving significance for us. Let us narrow our focus then, and speak just of Jesus' death/resurrection. If our analysis of the human predicament is correct, and sin and death are the core problems of the human situation, how does the death and resurrection of Jesus speak to these problems in a saving way?

Let us first consider sin. In the killing of the Son of God, human sinfulness reaches its peak. Here is a perfectly good and gentle person, engaged in a selfless ministry to suffering humanity, a merciful work of liberation. And they get him for it. Jealous, narrow-minded, self-serving people, far less beautiful and far less important, conspire against him and bring him down. As he falls, many who had belonged to him are shaken and lose their faith, and most of his closest personal friends flee the scene, embarrassed and fearful for themselves. One, in fact, is associated with the conspirators; another, under questioning, denies ever having known him. Religious and civic leaders cooperate in a rigged trial whose outcome is a foregone conclusion. And the death to which they subject him is deliberately punitive, both humiliating and painful. Human sinfulness is at work from the beginning to the end of this. Jesus is destroyed and buried. Then, most amazingly, he is raised. This could be good news or bad news. He appears in the upper room to those who had been his closest friends. What does he say to them? Does he say, "Where were you when I needed you, you hypocrites?" Or, "Peter, stand up and come here." Or, "If you thought God was angry about human sinfulness *before*, you should see God now!" No, he says, "Peace be with you." And, "Have you got anything to eat?" And then, breathing on them, "Receive the Holy Spirit." Was this amazing benevolence just for them? No. "Go out into the whole world and preach the good news to all creation." By saying things like these instead of what we should have expected him to say after what had happened, he spoke to our problems of sin and guilt in a perfectly astonishing way. He gave us the most unforgettable experience of the graciousness of God, the God who was in him. No longer could sin and guilt cause us to despair.

What about the problem of death? This problem too comes to a climax in the tragic death of Jesus. We know how our hearts react when we get news of the assassination of persons like John F. Kennedy, Martin Luther King, Malcolm X, Robert Kennedy, Anwar Sadat, and Mohandas Gandhi. We feel a tremendous sense of loss. We are outraged at the wrong of it, and begin to wonder whether good has a chance in the world, or whether the forces of evil are always stronger and in the end triumphant. At a radical level, we come up against the question of meaning. Imagine the experience of Jesus. He goes about doing good, following his call. With a deep sense of compassion for all human beings in their affliction, he labors to bring about a better world. His feeling is that he has just barely begun when he becomes aware of the forces of evil conspiring against him. He is seized and subjected to all that we are already familiar with, and breathes his last in the most excruciating pain, alone. What possible sense does this make? Is there a good God? If so, what is this God doing? This is death at its worst, death the end of everything. His life is simply wrested from him, no hand lifted in his defense. But then he is raised from death, making some appearances to his friends and other chosen witnesses. Again God has broken through the darkness. The God who seems to be absent when tragedy befalls us and wipes us out, absent or at least powerless, is mysteriously present and powerful deep inside it all. God is present and at work, bringing life out of death, good out of evil, and meaning out of absurdity. Even when death and absurdity seem most to be having their way, God is at work on our behalf prevailing against them. This is something terribly important to understand about God, and we experience it in the death and resurrection of Jesus.

This is the revelation that saves us, this experience of the kind of God we have. The twin evils of sin and death reach a climax in the tragic killing of Jesus, yet right here in his death and resurrection the presence and power of God are most powerfully felt. This experience saves us, because it entirely transforms our understanding and heals our hearts. No longer do we have to fear sin and death as we otherwise would, no longer do they darken the face of existence and drain our hearts of all energy. Christ is the light of the world, his Father the source of our hope.

THE SATISFACTION THEORY OF SALVATION

Let us contrast this interpretation of the death and resurrection of Jesus as salvation with an interpretation which has had a great deal of influence since the Middle Ages when Anselm of Canterbury first articulated it. This is the satisfaction theory of redemption. Its contours are probably familiar. The sin of Adam was an infinite offense against the majesty of God, infinite because it was an offense against God. It incurred God's wrath, and as a result human beings were no longer in God's grace and heaven was closed to them. The offense had to be repaired or atoned for. Because it was infinite, God would have to make the satisfaction for it; because it was committed by a human being, a human being would have to atone for it. Thus it required the God-man, the Second Person of the Blessed Trinity in human flesh, to repair the damage. By his death, his sacrifice for us as victim on the altar of the cross, the God-man atones for the sin of Adam and all subsequent human sins, and thus the wrath of God is turned away and we can again live in the grace of God in hope of heaven.

Influential as this theory of redemption has been, contemporary theologians have turned away from it as an adequate account of our salvation through Jesus Christ. They find it laboring under two immense difficulties: the image of God presented in it, and its variance with the New Testament emphasis on God as the one who takes all the initiative in our salvation.

The image of God in the satisfaction theory is of one whose anger will not be satisfied until the last penny is paid. There has to be a bloody sacrifice before there can be forgiveness. Someone has to die, and if it is not going to be the actual culprit, then it must be someone else. This is not a very flattering image of God. In the world of fallen human beings, many can do better than this when they are wronged. They simply say, "It's all right. I forgive you. No, it isn't necessary to make it up. Let's just forget it." How would we feel about the father of a family whose child had somehow wronged him, demanding the death of that child in satisfaction, or the death of a brother or sister in his stead? What would we think of that father if he took satisfaction in seeing his child suffer and die and in seeing it found his anger appeased? Yet the image of God in the satisfaction theory is precisely this. It would be difficult to love such a father, or even to respect him. And this image of God is radically at variance both with the faithful God of the Hebrew people and with the portrait of the Father Jesus paints for us in the parable of the prodigal son. That brings us to the second difficulty with the theory.

In the New Testament presentation of our salvation, it is God who takes all the initiative. Far from being an angry God awaiting the death of Jesus to turn again toward us, it is a solicitous and active God we see at work arranging our salvation.

> By this the love of God was made manifest among us, because God sent forth his only-begotten Son into the world that we might gain life through him (1 Jn 4:9).

> God was in Christ, reconciling the world to himself, not counting men's offenses against them, and he has entrusted to us this word of reconciliation (2 Cor 5:19).

> For God so loved the world that he gave his only-begotten Son, so that everyone who believes in him might not be destroyed but have everlasting life. For God sent his Son into the world not for him to judge the world, but for the world to be saved through him (Jn 3:16–17).

> If God is for us, who can be against us? He who did not even spare his own Son but handed him over for us all, why will he not also with him kindly give us all other things? Who will bring accusation against God's chosen ones? God is the one who declares them righteous. Who is he that will condemn? (Rom 8:31–34).

Jesus' parable of the prodigal son perfectly depicts who needs to be changed in the relationship between God and humanity. The parable portrays the sinful situation of any one of us who breaks off with God in search of greener pastures. In the story, it is not the father who is turned away; it is the son. The reconciliation takes place not when the father decides to forgive his son, but when the son decides to give up his wayward life and find his father again. As he turns his face toward home, he sees his father running toward him. And as he begins to unfold his speech of sorrow, he finds his father cutting him short and telling him to get ready for a party. According to the parable, and the whole gracious ministry of Jesus in God's name, the love of God is the constant dependable factor, and reconciliation takes place by its power when sinful human beings believe in it and receive it as the free gift that it is. Jesus is the one who, not for the first time in history, but again and most cogently, shows the quality of that love.

If, with most contemporary theologians, we abandon the satisfaction theory and understand how the life, death, and resurrection of Jesus are salvation for us along quite different lines, how are we to understand New Testament expressions which point toward Anselm's theory, expressions like "sacrifice," "by his blood," "died for our sins," "propitiation," "ransom for many," etc.? The key is to recognize that these expressions are metaphors. They are images pressed into service, along with many others, to express partial insights into the complex mystery of our salvation. Each catches a facet of it, by analogy with some familiar human experience. But every analogy is imperfect; the heart of it applies, while many of its particulars do not.

For example, Jesus' death is a *sacrifice*. He freely gives up his life out of love for God and human beings; in doing so, he willingly forfeits all that is most precious. That is a sacrifice if ever there was one. It is not a sacrifice because it is a bloody death, or because it takes place on some kind of altar, or because it appeases an angry God. Similarly, his *blood* is a symbol of the totality of his gift for us; it has no particular saving or healing significance other than that. Likewise, a kind of *redemption*, literally, a buying back, does take place. Jesus, in the labors of his life and death, does pay a heavy price. As a result we are freed from a bad situation, the slavery constituted by our sinful ways and their effects on the whole human situation. But this is a metaphor too. There is no literal paying of a blood price either to God or, in a still cruder interpretation, to the devil, to get us out of hell. We are transferred from one way of life to another, from one sort of experience to another, and the transfer is costly to the one who liberates us. The metaphor of *ransom* has essentially the same meaning. And Jesus does *die for our sins*, in two senses. He dies *because* of human sinfulness; it is human malice and wickedness that conspire to destroy him. And the entire way he lives and accepts his death *shows* us the only *way* that sin and sin's effects can be overcome in this broken world. Like him, we must bear the sins of many and be broken by them, not returning violence for violence in an endless cycle of revenge, but simply absorbing the evil and trusting our cause to God. When Jesus is lifted up on the cross in perfect helplessness, having no power but the naked power of truth and goodness, he draws us all to himself (Jn 12:32). He dies for our sins by suffering them and showing us the only way out of them. It is the great lesson of non-violence.

All the metaphors of salvation contain facets of the truth, and all require careful interpretation as metaphors. None fits perfectly. They must be explicated in a way that is consistent with the whole message of the New Testament. And they must be balanced off against each other in a mutually corrective way. Anselm focused on the metaphors of sacrifice and redemption and interpreted them according to some of the practices of medieval society. Theologians today view salvation much more as a matter of revelation and experience than as a transaction between Son and Father. No transaction was needed to change the Father's stance toward us, but we did need and always will need to see and experience the kind of love God has for us in the face of all sin and death. We also needed and will always need a human model of how we are called to live in a sinful and death-bound world. These are the gifts God has given us in Jesus Christ.

IN SUM

Although the death and resurrection of Jesus are pivotal for our salvation, they are not the only source of that salvation. Jesus' entire life, ministry, and teaching save us. His death/resurrection simply put it all in sharpest focus.

Everything Jesus undergoes in his death/resurrection, and all that is revealed in them, is already present in his teaching:

Do not fear those who kill the body (Mt 10).

Not a sparrow falls to the ground without your Father knowing (Mt 10).

In my Father's house there are many mansions (Jn 14).

There is no greater love than this, that someone lay down his life for a friend (Jn 15).

Blessed are you when people persecute you; your reward is great in heaven (Mt 5).

Love your enemies; pray for those who persecute you (Mt 5).

The death/resurrection exemplify the teaching, and do so dramatically, but they do not say anything brand new. And the teachings of Jesus in direct discourse and in parable are far more elaborate than the death/resurrection alone, even if they are not as eloquent. Jesus' death/resurrection are best understood in the light of all he taught. But his teaching, as we have it in the New Testament, is itself salvific, showing us the way. This is why Martha's sister Mary loved to sit at his feet, listening to him (Lk 10), and Peter said: "Lord, to whom shall we go? You have the words of eternal life" (Jn 6:68).

Jesus is the perfect embodiment of Gospel living, and this too is salvific for us. He *is* the word he teaches, which is why in the Fourth Gospel he is called the word of God (Jn 1). He *is* the good news. This lived example, the beauty and power of this man's life, inspire us and move us to deeds of greatness, and this too constitutes salvation.

The New Testament uses a variety of expressions to articulate the multi-faceted experience of salvation. Besides the term "salvation" itself, we find:

redemption	reconciliation
forgiveness of sins	justification
liberation or freedom	peace
adoption as God's children	sanctification
new creation	new life
healing	eternal life

This list is not exhaustive. Some of the terms stress the transformation of the individual, others the effect on human community. In the light of this richness, we can see yet more clearly what an impoverishment it is to equate salvation with satisfaction for sin through Jesus' death or simply with life after death.

Looking at one's own lived experience, and trying to articulate how Jesus saves or helps or heals, a person might say things like these:

He reveals who God is for me.
He teaches me what God wants from me.
He accepts me as I am, and gently moves me to grow.
He is my friend.

>He shows me what life is all about: union with God and loving
>   relationships with all people.
>He inspires me with courage and hope in the face of every
>   suffering.
>He forgives me.
>He is the resource I call on when I feel unequal.
>He is always with me.
>He promises me fuller life to come.
>He forms a community that helps me tremendously.

The human experience most helpful for understanding what Christian salvation is is the experience of love. When we are loved, we are saved. When we are loved, we come to life. Salvation is the experience of the love of God for us. This love experience is superior to all others, because it comes from God rather than from a human being, and so it is ultimate. And it is radically dependable; there is no chance that it will change or be removed. Even if all human love deserts me, this love will be there. Everything about me as a flawed human being is already known, and this love is given anyway. It reaches me in a human life, the life of Jesus of Nazareth, now the Christ risen in glory. This love tells me that reality is trustworthy, and that life has a happy ending.

How do we come in contact with this saving love? It reaches us in the New Testament, read privately or proclaimed and preached on. It reaches us in sacrament, Christ present in symbolic saving action. It comes to us in the community of Christians who constitute Christ's body in the world, in their words and deeds and in their love. And it touches us in that personal presence of Christ given to us with the gift of the Holy Spirit. This love enlivens and changes us, heals and strengthens us, empowers us to overcome sin in ourselves and in the structures of human society, and ushers us through that transition which opens out to the fullness of life, whose shape we cannot yet see. All this is what we mean by Christian salvation.

QUESTIONS FOR DISCUSSION

1. Why is salvation treated first in this book?
2. What are the principal things the world today needs to be saved from? Is Jesus any help?
3. What are the principal things you yourself need to be saved from? Is Jesus any help?
4. What relevance, if any, do the following items have in the human quest of salvation: forgiveness, community, heaven, understanding and attitude?
5. What do you think of the satisfaction theory of salvation?
6. How do the death and resurrection of Jesus save us? Do these alone constitute our salvation?
7. Where can one come in contact with the saving power of Jesus Christ?

II. Christian Discipleship

Jesus does not just save us. He calls us to follow him. He does not just comfort us; he challenges us as well. What Jesus began in his life is not yet finished. He inaugurated the reign of God, but he asks our help in bringing it to completion. The following of Jesus is called discipleship. A disciple is literally a learner or student. The call is to assimilate the teaching of Jesus and imitate his example. It is to labor with him for the transformation of the world.

Discipleship does not stand next to salvation as a separate topic. It stands within it. To live the Gospel is already to be saved in considerable measure. One has found the way, the truth, and the life. One knows the joy of Jesus in following his path, living in union with God in love. One is no longer lost, but has been found. No longer enslaved in habits of sinfulness, one has turned away from death to life. True, one is not completely saved. But Christian discipleship is the way which leads to life, both in this world and in the next. And Christian disciples help bring God's saving love to all humanity.

It is on Jesus that we must concentrate our attention if we wish to grasp the contours of Christian discipleship. He models the way of life, and he teaches it. Let us examine the main features of his life and teaching. Then let us look at some of the ways discipleship can go astray. Finally, let us speak of friendship with Jesus Christ as the heart of discipleship.

JESUS' LIFE

1. **He Lives for God.** The most striking feature of the life of Jesus is how totally centered it is in God. Out of his own

"Abba experience," which we will describe more fully later on, Jesus names God "Father," and draws close to him. This is the God Jesus wants to share with us. "Father" is a metaphor. It does not mean that God is masculine. The metaphor could as easily be "Mother." The God of Jesus is gentle, nurturing, faithful, tender, creative, compassionate. The idea of the metaphor, which arises from human experience, is that God is like a loving parent, the best conceivable, and that we can relate to God in love and trust, knowing that we are accepted and cared for. Jesus lives his whole life before this God. He trusts God, even when trust is hardest. He sees God's creative hand and providence everywhere. He speaks of God freely and often. He seeks opportunities to be alone with God in prayer. Jesus' whole objective is to do God's will, to accomplish God's work. It is interesting that the death of God movement in the 1960's found Jesus attractive and compelling apart from God, about whom it was reluctant to speak. Jesus *is* attractive and compelling as a human person, and probably almost everything about him would appeal to an atheist. But Jesus certainly cannot be explained, or even adequately described, without his relationship to God. God is everything to him.

2. **He Lives for Others.** Open the Gospel to almost any page, and you will find Jesus dealing with someone. It might be an individual, it might be a crowd, but in the scene Jesus is doing something for someone. He is forgiving sins, healing diseases, freeing people from their fears, feeding a crowd, calming a storm, teaching or answering questions, inviting or encouraging someone. He might also be confronting religious and political leaders, but even this will be in the interest of oppressed people. The Lutheran theologian Dietrich Bonhoeffer calls Jesus "the man for others." He is devoted to relieving human misery. He spends himself in service. What is amazing in Jesus is the universality of his love, his reverence for all persons no matter who they are, his ability to see the good, his de-

sire that all people enjoy inner and outer freedom and fullness of life.

When we look for cues as to how to live the Christian life, it is important to note that Jesus is a man in the midst. He is not an ascetic or a recluse. He leads no desert movement, and counsels no one to "leave the world," though he tells us we are not "of the world" (Jn 17:15–16). We find him in some Gospel frames seeking lonely places to be with God, but always he returns to service, which remains the dominant note. His prayer seems to serve his ministry, even that longest prayer of his, the forty days in the desert, from which he emerges to begin his public life. In his public life Jesus is chided for not fasting, as John the Baptist and his disciples fast. He earns instead the name of "glutton and drunkard, friend of tax collectors and sinners" (Lk 7:34) for his practice of eating and drinking with the despised of his time. By contrast, he is never cited for feats of asceticism, nor is his celibacy made anything of, either by himself or by his contemporaries. The focus is elsewhere, on his love and service of people, flowing from his relationship with God.

3. **He Is the Sacrament of God's Presence, Love, and Power.** "Emmanuel" is what Matthew's Gospel calls Jesus, "God with us" (Mt 1:23). That is how people experience him. John's Gospel calls him "the Word," a term with a rich background in the Hebrew Scriptures. The Hebrew people knew God to be self-communicating, and everything they heard from God, whether in nature, in historical events, or in prophetic spokespersons, they called God's word. Applying this pregnant term to Jesus means that all God wants to communicate to humankind is gathered right here, in this man, not just in his words but in his whole personhood. It means that Jesus is a sacrament, for sacramentality is nothing else but making the invisible visible. "The person who sees me sees the Father" (Jn 14:9).

The most striking experience of God's gracious outreach in Jesus was his table fellowship with sinners. In this good man's acceptance of them, people experienced God's own acceptance, forgiveness, and affirmation. It gave them a new lease on life. This entire Gospel tradition of gracious hosting is the background of our Eucharist.

Jesus' outreach has other forms too, as in the calling of poor fishermen, talking at length with a woman drawing water, inviting Zacchaeus to come down from his tree and host him, raising the son of the widow of Naim, accepting the hospitality and friendship of Martha and Mary. The response of people to Jesus shows that in him they recognize the sacrament of God: present, loving, powerful against everything that blocks access to life.

It is in this sacramentality of his to others that the first two outstanding features of Jesus' life converge. He reaches out to others as an overflow of his union with God, who sends him to humanity out of the divine love. As Jesus serves people in a human way, they experience the God who fills him.

4. **Jesus Is Free.** The personality of Jesus is original. He is his own person. His replies to questions are fresh, unexpected. His parables are ingenious. His responses to situations are always surprising, e.g., when he deals with the tax due to Caesar (Mk 12), with the woman who washes his feet with her tears (Lk 7), with the Pharisees' demand for a sign (Mk 8). The great bulk of his teaching is his own, showing fresh departures, winning admiration (Mt 7).

Jesus is free from other people's expectations. He will not accommodate Herod with a miracle even to save his life (Lk 23), will not let the people make him king (Jn 6), will not resort to violence though violence is used against him (Mt 26). His relatives come to take him away because they think he is mad (Mk 3). His own brothers do not believe in him (Jn 7). His disciples frequently show misunderstanding and disagreement, and Peter challenges him directly (Mk 8). But Jesus stays the course, even when it is a very lonely one.

He is free from the law and the tradition. He is respectful of both, and lives by and large within them. But he does not hesitate to set them aside when he sees a greater value. So he sets aside the sabbath observance to help someone in need, sets aside capital punishment to save a woman caught in adultery, sets aside fasting in the interest of table fellowship. Many of Jesus' actions would be called civil disobedience today. His was a society in which religious law and civil law were one. So it was civil disobedience to touch a leper, to eat with tax collectors, to release an adulteress from the death penalty, to heal or to take grain from the fields on the sabbath, to exempt oneself from fasting laws. But Jesus lived a set of values which sometimes required civil disobedience.

Jesus was free from possessions. He was an itinerant preacher, with no place to lay his head. He depended upon the hospitality of others. At his death, there was nothing to divide up except one garment.

Jesus was free from fear. He could not be bought off. Not that he did not feel fear. He felt it keenly, but he would not be governed by it. He continued to do the good and to speak the truth in the face of every threat—of arrest, of calumny, of death. Threats availed nothing with him.

JESUS' TEACHING

We have looked at some of the outstanding features of Jesus' life. What did he teach? His life and teaching are of a piece. He teaches the same values that he lives.

1. **The Love of God.** God is for us. We can trust God, because God knows what we need before we ask (Mt 6). The very hairs of our heads are numbered (Mt 10). We can rely on God's

love in spite of sin and failure, because God is compassionate (Lk 6). Indeed, God's mercy is seen in action in the public ministry of Jesus, the image of God (2 Cor 5), who reaches out to sinners. God's will has a sovereign claim on us. It is summed up in Jesus' great commandment: love of God and love of neighbor (Mt 22). We love God because God has first loved us. Much of Jesus' teaching is directed to reimaging God for us as loving parent, with all that follows from that understanding.

2. **Love of Neighbor.** Jesus lays great stress on our relationships with one another, and here too what he teaches is what he lives. Our love should extend to all, even to those who hate us, malign us, oppress or persecute us. We should pray for them, and do good to them (Mt 5). We should love the sinner. Jesus teaches us to forgive injuries, after the model of God's forgiveness of our sins (Mt 18). We are supposed to forgive the same injury, even if it occurs again and again (Mt 18). Jesus teaches us to love the poor, even to the extent of selling all we have and giving it to them (Mk 10). His parable of the good Samaritan tells us to help those who need help, even if we do not know them, or if their path crosses ours at a most inconvenient time (Lk 10). We should feed the hungry, give drink to the thirsty, welcome the stranger, clothe the naked, visit those who are ill or in prison (Mt 25). We should serve one another, even to washing one another's feet (Jn 13).

Jesus offers two different standards for measuring whether our love for others is what it should be. One is that we love others the way we love ourselves (Mt 22). The other is that we love one another the way Jesus loves us (Jn 13). The detail in which Jesus draws out this teaching makes it clear that he has something different from a general sentiment in mind. "I love humanity," Charlie Brown says. "It's people I can't stand." In Jesus' teaching, it is the neighbor, not humanity, who is to be loved, the person who is there in the flesh, not the abstraction.

3. **Simplicity of Life.** Jesus tells us not to lay up treasure for ourselves on earth (Mt 6). He insists that we cannot serve God and mammon (Mt 6). He calls the poor blessed, and pronounces woes on the rich (Lk 6). In a paradigmatic encounter, he tells a rich young man that he should sell all he has and follow him (Mk 10). He says that it is easier for a camel to get through the eye of a needle than for a rich person to enter God's kingdom (Mk 10). In a parable he depicts a man who is busy building himself bigger barns, and calls him a fool (Lk 12). His parable of the rich man and poor Lazarus puts Lazarus in the bosom of Abraham and the rich man in Hades (Lk 16).

These are not Jesus' best loved teachings in the West today, where Christians enjoy affluence. It is hard to know how to live them. But it is impossible to deny or minimize them, given their frequency in the Gospels. Jesus talked about riches and poverty more than about almost any other subject, including heaven and hell, sex, divorce, Church authority, or the law. One out of every ten verses in the first three Gospels is about rich and poor, one out of seven in Luke. Even in the Hebrew Scriptures, this is the second most common theme, the first being the related theme of idolatry.

Why such centrality? Probably for two reasons. The first is that where our treasure is, our heart is too (Mt 6). It is very hard to serve both God and mammon. The other is the plight of needy brothers and sisters, for whom also God wants life. Part of the contemporary realization is that giving a beggar a quarter does not sufficiently answer the commandment. This is how politics and economics have found their way into the pulpit, against some people's objections. In a world in such dire economic imbalance, in which a small percentage of wealthy people enjoy so much while such masses of people struggle for bare existence and often lose the battle to disease or starvation, Jesus' teaching challenges the very structure of national and world economies. This situation is incompatible with the reign of God. Figuring out how to redistribute the goods of the earth in response to the love commandment is one of the great challenges of our day.

4. **An Attitude to Suffering.** Jesus' own efforts to ease people's burdens, and his sending of his disciples to do the same, indicates where he stands on the question of human suffering. His first response to it is to struggle against it, to eradicate or lessen it. And if we see in him what God is doing and wants done, then we also know where God stands on human suffering. God's cause is the human cause. God wants life for us, not death. Jesus points to the fruits of his labors as the sign that the reign of God is taking over: the blind see, the lame walk, lepers are cleansed, the dead are raised, and the poor have good news preached to them (Mt 11). What Jesus says of evil in the world, both as sin and as suffering, is that "an enemy has done this" (Mt 13:28). Exactly who or what that enemy is is difficult to construe, but it is clear from this parable of the wheat and the weeds that the master of the field sowed good seed, not weeds. And what this means for our present purposes is that God labors with us, not against us, as we strive to overcome sin and suffering. So our first response to suffering is to resist and eradicate it. On this the whole healing ministry of the Church is based.

The second response to suffering comes only after we have done all we can to overcome it. It is to accept the unsolved remainder in hope. It is to trust in God, whose power goes beyond our own and often works secretly. Jesus himself resists death until he cannot anymore. He slips through the crowd that would throw him over the mountainside (Lk 4:30), and avoids being seen in public when his enemies are lying in wait (Jn 11:54). But when his hour comes, he accepts the suffering and death that come to him, placing his trust in God.

Everything that Jesus teaches about trust in God in the face of life's difficulties grounds this second response to suffering: accept the unsolved remainder in hope.

There are two pitfalls into which Christian discipleship falls in this matter of suffering. One is to seek suffering for its own sake, as if it had the highest value. The other is to seek joy, trying to avoid all suffering. Both are mistakes. In the teaching of Jesus, suffering and joy are by-products, never the object of direct seeking. The object of direct seeking in the Gospel is to do the good, to live the truth, to love God and neighbor. If we dedicate our lives to these goals, we will suffer. And we will have joy. They are both accompaniments of Gospel living, as they were both accompaniments of Jesus' life. Jesus knows great suffering and deep joy, but he does not directly seek either. His eyes are fixed on other goals.

Before we leave this summary of what Jesus lived and taught, we would do well to notice an item which did not make the summary—sex. Sex did not make the summary because it is at best a minor key in the life and teaching of Jesus. This is worth remarking because so often when the Christian life is presented, sexual prohibitions are a prominent part of the presentation. Indeed, the popular image of the Church is that of an institution negatively preoccupied with sex—no "impure thoughts," no masturbation, no homosexuality, no extramarital sex, no birth control. All those in prominent positions in the Roman Catholic Church are celibate. The statement is really quite resounding in both its verbal and non-verbal aspects.

If Jesus had shown a negative attitude toward sexuality, his community should too. But that is the anomaly. He did not. Sex is a subject on which Jesus says very little—nothing on masturbation, homosexuality, premarital sex, or birth control. He speaks against adultery, but that involves a significant breach of covenant. He proposes an ideal of purity of heart, but it is recorded in only one Gospel, and that in only one line (Mt 5:28). Jesus himself is apparently celibate, but he makes nothing of it. And when he deals with anyone who has gone wrong sexually, he simply forgives the person, no questions asked. The Gospels hardly constitute a basis for the Church's preoccupation with sex. Responsible sexuality is, of course, a Christian concern, because it pertains to loving. All that is being asserted here is that the issue has loomed far too large in proportion to the attention Jesus gave it.

THE "SPIRITUAL LIFE"

When people begin to think about the spiritual life, which is another way of speaking of discipleship, somehow they lose their way. They forget the main emphases of the Gospel, and lapse into religiosity. The initial mistake may lie in speaking of "the spiritual life" in the first place. Jesus just talks about life.

Yet somehow when people think about practicing their faith more earnestly, they resolve on the following: they will meditate everyday, they will go more frequently to the Eucharist, they will seek sacramental reconciliation regularly, they will get themselves a spiritual director, they will join a prayer group, they will increase their devotions, they will undertake fasting or some other penance, they will do more spiritual reading, and they will talk religiously. This seems like a serious spiritual program, the way to follow Jesus, become holy, and get close to God.

I can think of a number of people I have known who have done all these things and yet do not really live the Gospel. They have never been converted, though they are religiously very active and their talk is unmistakably religious. What are they missing?

To answer that we have to take a look at what is really wrong with human beings, what stands in need of radical conversion. There are several things.

1. **We do not trust God.** We do not really believe that God loves us, because there are too many things wrong with us. Not only do we not believe that we are accepted and even cherished for who we are, but we do not trust in God's care for us either. We figure that we had better make provision for the morrow, or the morrow will surely destroy us. We are anxious about many things, quite sure they will not work out. We do not trust God.

2. **We do not like ourselves.** We beat on ourselves constantly. We put ourselves down. We screen out affirmation, and nurse the remarks that hurt us. We compare ourselves unfavorably with others. We are well aware of all that is wrong with us, and acknowledge almost none of our gifts. We withhold ourselves from others, figuring that we have nothing to offer, and that if we let them know us they would most likely reject us. We have already rejected ourselves.

3. **We do not like other people.** Oh, we do like certain ones. But we do not like most of them. We don't like women, or we don't like men. We don't like chicanos, or maybe it's blacks, polacks, orientals, or Jews. We don't like commies, or queers, or hippies, or maybe we don't like straights or squares. Much of it is fear. We have never met one, and do not want to take the chance. We hang on to our grudges too, against aunts and uncles, parents, children, even those with whom we share bed and board. Thank God there are a few people we can love. But sometimes they are hard to find.

4. **We seek happiness and security in wealth and power.** We want to be comfortable. We want to cut a successful figure in the world, to command respect. We want to grab all the gusto we can get, and be on easy street tomorrow. A good dog or two should be able to guard our possessions, backed

up by a small handgun. Against larger numbers, some well placed nuclear warheads should do the trick. To live is to have many things, and to be safe is to be fully insured and well defended.

In sum, we are selfish and prejudiced, hard-hearted and closed-minded. We are judgmental and unforgiving. And often we are sorry we are alive. We do not view life as a gift and an opportunity, but see it as a burden and a drag, complaining about how awful it is or how bored we are. These are the things that are wrong with us. These are the things that need to change.

Jesus offers to heal our diseases, with his life, his teaching, and his gift of the Holy Spirit. The process requires our cooperation. Almost always in the Gospel, Jesus required the cooperation of the patient in a healing. They had to take up their bed and walk (Mk 2), go and show themselves to the priest (Lk 10), go and wash in the pool (Jn 9). The spiritual healing we all need entails a transformation of all our relationships: to God, to ourselves, to others, to things. The changing of our relationships changes us, for we are constituted the persons we are precisely by our relationships. But we have to cooperate with the Lord's action.

1. **He changes our relationship to God.** He puts us into a relationship of love with God. He teaches us that God is compassionate and merciful, and accepts us as we are. He teaches and shows us that God can be trusted to take care of us.

2. **He changes our relationship to ourselves.** By his love and reverence for each person, even the most abandoned or unpromising, he shows us that we are good. Are we any worse than the people in the Gospels? God's acceptance of us in Jesus becomes the basis for our self-acceptance. It is all right to be imperfect, limited, in process. It is all right to fall, if we are just willing to get up again.

3. **He changes our relationship to others.** He tells us to love, and shows us how to do it, and gives us his Spirit to empower us. He teaches and models the path of reconciliation. He shows us that we find life and God not in isolation but in involvement, in our relationships with one another. He teaches us something about buried treasure, which the English essayist, G.K. Chesterton, puts most aptly. According to Greek legend, a man by the name of Diogenes went about the world with a lantern, looking for a just man; he could not find one. Chesterton says Jesus found him—inside the good thief.

4. **He changes our relationship to things.** He teaches and models simplicity of life, the opposite of acquisitiveness, and tells us that if someone steals something from us we should give that person more besides (Mt 5:38–42). Not only does he teach this sort of *freedom* from things; he teaches us a *contemplative attitude* toward them as well. All of his teachings are derived from the ordinary things of the world—seed and harvest, the seasons, children, banquets and weddings, birds and lilies, sheep and shepherds. In all things Jesus sees the creative and generous hand of God, and in nature he reads the parables of God. If he can see these things, perhaps we can learn to see them too.

This is how we are healed, through this transformation of all our relationships, which brings with it the transformation of ourselves. This is Christian discipleship and Christian spirituality. It is also salvation, at least the first installment on it.

What is the relationship between these demanding transformations of our selfhood and the religious practices we enumerated earlier—the meditation, sacraments, prayer group, etc.? They sustain the Christian life. It is very difficult to keep Christian values in focus, and to live the demands of discipleship, if we do not read Scripture, pray, and lean on other Christians for support and direction. The culture does not encourage us. We need reminders, symbols, stories, exhortations, living models, times out for reflection, and times for celebration. These things are indispensable supports. The error is to think that these things *are* the Christian life. Just as Jesus' practice of prayer was in the service of his whole way of life, a means rather than an end, so must ours be. It was his whole life that was his worship of God. So must ours be. Insofar as prayer, sacraments, reading, and spiritual direction support genuine Christian living, i.e., Christian attitudes, relationships, choices, and action, they are useful. When they become an escape from the more difficult demands of Christian living, they are the corruption of discipleship. The question at the last judgment is not "How religious was your talk?" nor "How much time did you spend in prayer?" nor "Was your faith orthodox in every respect?" It is, rather, "How did you respond to needy brothers and sisters?" (Mt 25). That is one reliable measure of our discipleship. Paul offers a more elaborate set of criteria: charity, joy, peace, patience, mildness, generosity, long-suffering, and self-control (Gal 5:22–23).

FRIENDSHIP WITH JESUS CHRIST

Jesus is not just a teacher, nor just a model for us to imitate. Jesus still lives, and he offers himself to each of us as companion and friend. This is a very important aspect of Christian discipleship, and the New Testament lays a great deal of stress on it.

And know that I am with you always, even till the end of the world (Mt 28:20).

Anyone who loves me will be true to my word, and my Father will love him; we will come to him and make our dwelling place with him (Jn 14:23).

> Here I stand, knocking at the door. If anyone hears me
> calling and opens the door, I will enter his house, and dine
> with him (Rev 3:20).

> No longer do I call you servants; I have called you friends
> (Jn 15:15).

This personal relationship with Christ is a very attractive
and comforting aspect of Christian spirituality. It takes some of
the work out of it. It gives one a companion and friend in all
seasons, all circumstances. Such friendship is different from
ordinary human friendships in that this friend is not visible or
tangible. He is also a more exalted friend, God with us. Yet a
genuine friendship with him is possible, because he is present
to us, is interested in us, and does want to share with us. These
are the essential ingredients of a friendship.

St. Paul's whole life is based on his friendship with Jesus
Christ. We see the same thing in many of the later saints. Paul
says, "For me, to live is Christ" (Phil 1:21). Paul turns his
whole life over to Christ, trusts him, thinks about him, praises
him, asks him for what he needs, conceives all his lifework in
terms of Christ, and gratefully receives the constant love of
Christ. "He loved me and gave himself up for me" (Gal 2:20).
This is the idea. Paul's oft repeated expression for the Christian life is life "in Christ." He is a fine example of that kind of
living Jesus speaks of in his farewell discourse.

> I am the vine; you are the branches. The person who lives
> in me and I in him will produce abundantly, for apart from
> me you can do nothing (Jn 15:5).

Paul puts it this way: "I can do all things in him who strengthens me" (Phil 4:13).

All of us need this kind of resource, and it is offered to us.

What do we have to do to establish this relationship? Nothing more than ask for it, and open our hearts to receive it. But we must seriously want Christ in our lives. We have to be willing to turn our lives over to him in trust and obedience, imitating the way he turned his life over in trust and obedience to his Father. The friendship we are speaking of here is not given once and for all. Like all other friendships, it is a living reality. It requires tending or it dies. But if it is tended through the exercise of sharing, of giving and receiving in all those ways that Paul, for example, exercised it, then it grows, and we ourselves grow increasingly into the image of Christ. Ephesians sums it up in the form of a prayer.

> May Christ dwell in your hearts through faith, and may charity be the root and foundation of your life. Thus you will be able to grasp fully, with all the saints, the breadth and length and height and depth of Christ's love, and experience this love which surpasses all knowledge, so that you may attain to all the fullness of God (Eph 3:17–19).

We opened with the experience of salvation, the first experience which resulted from the encounter with Jesus. Now we have considered the demands of discipleship, drawing on the life and teaching of Jesus for our norms. This puts us in a position to raise the question which the first disciples raised as they tasted salvation and tried to live the sublime vision Jesus set before them: Who is this man who has so utterly changed our lives? Let us turn our attention now to that question.

QUESTIONS FOR DISCUSSION

1. What are the outstanding features of Jesus' life? Would you add others to those mentioned in this chapter?

2. What are the main emphases of Jesus' teaching? Would you add others to those mentioned in this chapter?
3. What does Christian discipleship require of us?
4. What is the relationship between discipleship and salvation?
5. What is the difference between Christian discipleship and religiosity? What is the relationship between religious activities and a way of life patterned on the Gospel?
6. Is there such a thing as a personal relationship with Jesus Christ? What does it mean? How is it initiated? How does it grow?

III. Chalcedon—Its Strengths and Limitations

It might seem strange to take our question about the identity of Jesus first to the Council of Chalcedon, which met in 451 A.D. Would we not be better advised to take it to the New Testament itself? In a way we would, because the New Testament is the first and ultimate norm of our faith. One problem is that in the New Testament there are many answers to the question, not just one. From the very beginning, the disciples of Jesus struggled with the question of his identity, and they gave it various answers. Jesus attracted to himself all the human titles of honor and divinity that existed or could be imagined in the time of imperial Rome: Just One, Holy One, Master, Prophet, Messiah (or Christ), Savior, Lord, Rabbi, Son of David, Son of God, Son of man, Word of God, and others, some fifty of them in all. The process began with the astonishment he caused in his public life, and continued with the further astonishment he caused by his resurrection. This process is called Christology, and it goes on in every age: Who is this man, and what is his significance for human history? As Roman Catholic New Testament scholars Joseph Fitzmyer and Raymond Brown point out, each of the four Gospels answers the question in a somewhat different way, and the writers of the Epistles in yet other ways, and sometimes various Christologies appear in the same document. It is in the nature of the question itself to defy some final, exhaustive answer.

In the fifth century of the Christian era, an ecumenical council was called to deal with the question because debate continued to rage in a lively way among various schools of thought. The terms of the question had shifted somewhat from New Testament times. It was now the late Roman Empire, and Greek philosophy had established the prevailing patterns of thought. As the question was debated now, it was debated in Greek rather than Hebrew terms, and the answer that was agreed upon at Chalcedon (though not all present agreed with it) was a Greek answer to the question. There is no way to escape the influence of culture. Culture constitutes a milieu, and we cannot but think in its terms.

WHAT THE COUNCIL DEFINED

The Council of Chalcedon was the most important of the early Christological councils. Its definitions, whatever their cultural limitations, have had a decisive influence on the Christological faith of succeeding generations right down to our own. It is Chalcedon which has given us the phrases "two natures in one person" and "true God and true man." These phrases have become such commonplaces in Christian discourse that many might think they are in the New Testament itself. They are not. They come to us from the Council of Chalcedon.

The full history of the Council is written up in many places, delineating the principal schools of thought that met there, the leading figures, the debates. Without going into all of that here, we just wish to indicate some of the Council's main concerns and then look at what it defined. What the Council was concerned to do was to create some kind of synthesis of the three factors of the problem: the human element in Jesus, the divine element in him, and the unity of his personality. They wanted to be careful not to emphasize either the human or the divine element at the expense of the other, and also not to suggest that Jesus was a split personality. There are probably many ways of accomplishing such a task, even though it is difficult, and there were already many proposals in the air at the time of the Council. The way that the Council chose finally to synthesize the competing proposals was in the following terms:

> In imitation of the holy Fathers we confess that our Lord Jesus Christ is one and the same Son . . . ; the same perfect in his divinity and the same perfect in his humanity;
>
> truly God and the same truly man of a rational soul and a body;
>
> of one nature with the Father according to the divinity, and the same of one nature with us according to the humanity, in all things like us except in sin;
>
> before the ages begotten of the Father according to the divinity, but the same in the last days, for us and for our salvation, (born) according to the humanity of Mary the Virgin and Mother of God;
>
> one and the same Christ, Lord, Only-begotten, in two natures;
>
> without confusion, without change, without division, and without separation.
>
> The difference of the natures is not removed through the union but, rather, the property of each nature is preserved and they coalesce in one person (*prosopon*) and one independence (*hypostasis*);
>
> not divided or separated into two persons,
>
> but one and the same only-begotten Son, God-Word, Jesus Christ the Lord (DS 301–302).

Though we may not be familiar with most of this statement, we are well acquainted with the substance of it. Its best known brief phrases have already been singled out. We might note two further points which flow from the statement in a determinative way for classical Christology. First, in Chalcedon and the theological development that flows from it, Jesus is called "man" in the generic sense (human), but not "a man." He has a human nature, but is not a human person. The person in him is the second person of the Blessed Trinity. Jesus does not have a human personal center. This is how the Council gets around the possible problem of a split personality.

Second, being God, Jesus has all the divine attributes. The definition does not state this, but subsequent theology developed it as a logical conclusion from the definition. If Jesus is truly God, then he must be all-powerful, all-knowing, and omnipresent. Also, if he is truly God, he knows this fact about himself throughout his human life. Besides this, he enjoys the immediate vision of God (beatific vision) all through his life. Finally, if he is truly God, then, though he is tempted, he cannot sin, for this would be absurd. All these conclusions follow deductively from the fundamental premise that Jesus is truly God, of one nature or substance with the Father.

The Council of Chalcedon is a monument in the history of theological reflection on Jesus, and any subsequent Christology must be in respectful dialogue with it even if it goes beyond it or tries to say the same essential things in a different way. Among the important legacies of the Council are its clarity and its strong insistence on both the divine and the human elements in Jesus, as well as on his personal unity. The Council enunciates unmistakably that it is God, nothing less, that we encounter in Jesus of Nazareth. The definitions of this early Council are accepted by all the major Christian denominations, and carry the weight of long tradition.

But every human statement is historically situated, and

the times do change. Chalcedon was itself a reformulation of New Testament expressions, thought to be better suited to the fifth century. St. Thomas Aquinas did another major reformulation of Christian faith in the thirteenth century, using the categories of Aristotelian philosophy. He was regarded as highly innovative, and aroused much official Church concern at the time. He was even summoned to Rome to answer questions. But as time went on he came to be regarded as *the* theologian of the Roman Catholic Church. In the present century, theologians again see the need for reformulation. The motivation is the same: to make the essential content of Christian faith more intelligible and more credible to the people of our time, and to draw out its important implications for the problems and questions we face today. Let us first examine the shortcomings that many theologians today find in the Chalcedonian model. Then in the next chapter let us look at their attempts at a reformulation better suited to the present age.

THE CONTEMPORARY CRITIQUE OF CHALCEDON

1. **Divine nature and human nature cannot be set side by side and numbered as if they were similar quantities.** The formula suggests that we know what human nature is, and that is questionable. It also suggests that we know what divine nature is, and that is even more questionable. Then it suggests that we can lay them side by side and number them as if they were in series, saying, as the Council says, that there are two of them and that they are not confused or changed by their coexistence in one person.

The Dutch Roman Catholic theologian Piet Schoonenberg points out that in most of our experience, the way God relates to the world is by working *within* created things. God operates through the powers of the created thing itself. God's presence in the beauty of the rose is in the rose's own beauty. It is expressed through it, not added to it as something in its own kind. It is always there, and always hidden, and yet also always partly revealed in the created thing's own presentation of itself to us. God's presence in the beauty of a human being like you or me is not a separate beauty which belongs to God and not to you or me, but a beauty that comes through us and is also really our own. God's presence in us is expressed completely in human terms. God is the source of our being, but works within us in such a way that we can be fully and freely ourselves, without interference or any violation of our own nature. Similarly, when God heals someone, God does not intervene and work independently of the ordinary created agencies at work, e.g., antibodies, doctors, medicines, physical therapy, but works from within those agencies, enabling them to be most powerfully themselves.

Now, if God works with Jesus in the same way, then the divinity of Jesus is going to appear precisely in his humanity, and be expressed only in a human mode. It is not going to lie alongside it, either operating independently, or so altering Jesus' humanity that it is a humanity unlike that of the rest of us. This brings us to the next objection.

2. **The Chalcedonian formula makes a genuine humanity impossible.** The conciliar definition says that Jesus is true man. But if there are two natures in him, it is clear which will dominate. And Jesus becomes immediately very different from us. He is omniscient, omnipotent, omnipresent. He knows past, present, and future, and enjoys the unbroken vision of God. He knows exactly what everyone is thinking and going to do. This is far from ordinary human experience. Jesus is tempted, but cannot sin because he is God. What kind of temptation is this? Can it be called temptation at all? It has little in common with the kinds of struggles we are familiar with.

These difficulties flow from the divinity overshadowing the humanity, and from Jesus not having a human personal center.

The formula explicitly assigns Jesus a human nature, and all Christians confess that Jesus is truly man as well as truly God. But if we consult our image of him, we recognize that we see him as a divine rather than a human being. His outward appearance is human, but his inner life is very different. He has a human body, and he eats, sleeps, and talks like a human person. But things are quite different within, where the self-consciousness is all that of God. Is it having a body, and eating and sleeping, that constitute a human being? What contemporary theologians are saying is that it is precisely the "innards" of a person that bear the distinctive marks of a human nature. The Anglican theologian John Knox puts this matter particularly well. To be human is to be inwardly human, and that is to be limited in knowledge, not to know the future, not to know what is inside others but only to be able to intuit or guess. To be inwardly human is to wonder who one is and what one is supposed to do with one's life, and to carry that question with varying degrees of acuity all through one's existence. To be human is to struggle with God, to be aware of God as present to oneself at times, but to know times too when God seems to be absent and out of reach. To be human is to unfold step by step in the recognition and realization of one's authentic selfhood (which includes one's vocation), not to possess it all at once from the beginning. Can Jesus be true God and at the same time be truly human in these essential ways?

We can see the same difficulty if we consider our living of the Christian life. The Christian spirituality that follows from Chalcedon has always been strong in this respect, that it brings God nearer, in Jesus, and so facilitates our relating to God. But in another respect, this spirituality has always been weak. We cannot identify with this Jesus. He is not just superior to us, the way St. Francis of Assisi was superior to most of us; he is different. He has not struggled in the mire of life the way we have to. So if we say to someone who is struggling to integrate his sexuality into responsible loving: "You know, Jesus had to struggle with this too," the person will probably respond: "What makes you think that? He was God." And if we say to the patient dying a painful death, with much fear and little sense of the presence of God: "It was in circumstances just like this, and with very similar feelings, that Jesus died," the patient will probably reply: "I know he suffered a lot. But he knew he was God and he knew he would rise again." If we try to console the person whose spouse has had an affair, who has been deeply wounded and cannot find it in her heart to forgive or trust again, and we say: "You know, Jesus didn't just talk about forgiving; he suffered some terrible hurts and betrayals from those who were closest, and had to struggle just as you do to forgive and trust them again," the person's likely reply would be: "But he was so different, and his whole life so different, that I just can't relate to what you are saying." In other words, Jesus is human in a way, but not in the way we are. And yet does not Hebrews say of him: "Since he was himself tested through what he suffered, he is able to help those who are tempted" (Heb 2:18)?

3. **The Chalcedonian formula has a meager basis in Scripture.** The Council calls Jesus true God. The New Testament shies away from calling Jesus God. The American Roman Catholic Scripture scholar, Raymond Brown, points out that in the entire New Testament Jesus is clearly called "God" only three times: John 1:14 (in conjunction with John 1:1), John 20:28, and Hebrews 1:8. All three of these are late New Testament writing, refer to the risen Christ rather than the Jesus of the public ministry, and are the faith confessions of others rather than of Jesus himself. If Jesus ever called *himself* God, the American Roman Catholic Scripture scholar Joseph Fitz-

myer observes, we have no record of it. But even the disciples, whether in the Gospels or in other New Testament writings, very rarely call Jesus God. He is commonly called Christ, Messiah, Son of man, Son of God, Savior, Rabbi, Lord, etc., but only three times clearly "God" in the twenty-seven books of the New Testament. When the New Testament uses the term "God," and it does so with very great frequency, the name designates the Father, not Jesus.

This is not at all to say that it is false to call Jesus God, or that the New Testament is a stranger to what Chalcedon asserts about Jesus. The intimate relationship between Jesus and God is found on practically every page of the New Testament. Jesus is the one sent by God, the Son of God, the one who forgives sins and teaches with divine authority. But the New Testament and Chalcedon speak about him in quite different languages, reflecting the difference between the Hebrew and Greek minds. The New Testament does not speak of two natures in one person, or do anything nearly as philosophically precise as the Council of Chalcedon does. These are categories of Greek, not of Hebrew, thought. Granted that there is some Greek influence already present in the New Testament, the Hebrew mentality which lies at the basis of the New Testament writings thought functionally, not ontologically. That is, it was more interested in what a thing *did* than in how it was *put together*. The Hebrew Scriptures described what God was doing, not what the nature of God was. The New Testament described what Jesus was doing in the name of God, not what the ontological constitution of Jesus was. Chalcedon put the question about Jesus' identity in a Greek manner, and gave it a Greek answer. It represents a considerable translation of what is found in the New Testament. There may be other ways of construing how Jesus was constituted which would equally well explain Jesus' ability to do what he did.

The New Testament offers a meager basis for saying that

Jesus was omnipotent, omniscient, omnipresent, or incapable of wrongdoing. We find works of power in the Gospels, but this is far from omnipotence, which is nowhere ascribed to Jesus. Regarding his knowledge, it is represented as limited. He did not know when the end of the world was coming (Mk 13:32), or even who touched him in a crowd of people (Mk 5:30). Raymond Brown points out that Jesus' exegesis of the Old Testament betrays the inadequate and even mistaken ideas of his generation where authorship, historicity, literary form, and principles of hermeneutics are concerned. Jesus' notions of demonology, apocalyptic, and the afterlife do not go beyond those of his time. In other areas he showed himself remarkably enlightened, e.g., where God's demands were concerned, or his own mission. But this is quite a different matter from omniscience. Nor does anything in Jesus' public life suggest that he was omnipresent. He is never represented as being present anyplace other than where he was physically.

The Jesus of the New Testament is genuinely tempted. His patience is sorely tried by the disciples' lack of understanding. He is tempted by the devil in the desert. He is tempted to turn away from the death he understands the Father to be asking of him. He seems tempted to despair on the cross. Hebrews tells us that "in the days of his flesh he cried aloud with tears to him who could save him from death" (Heb 5:7), and that, in general, "he has been tempted in every way just as we are, but without sin" (Heb 4:15). All this testimony squares poorly with the notion of a Jesus who because he is God *cannot* sin. The New Testament does say in a few places besides Hebrews that Jesus *did not* sin (e.g., Jn 8:46, 2 Cor 5:21), but that is a quite different assertion.

As Jesus dies on the cross, he cries out: "My God, my God, why have you forsaken me?" (Mk 15:34). This squares poorly with the notion that he was always possessed of the beatific vision. And if he was so possessed, his suffering and death are quite a different experience from the ordinary human experience of the same things. This recalls an earlier point.

4. **The Chalcedonian formula strains credulity in the modern world.** The Christology of Chalcedon is what is called a "descending" Christology. It starts in the bosom of the Trinity in heaven, with the decision of the second person to descend to earth and become man. God "comes down to save us." God "walks the lanes of Nazareth in human form." To many today, this sounds interesting but incredible. The type of thinking it represents simply does not square with our worldview, and is very difficult to take seriously. In our age, an "ascending" Christology is much more congenial to many. An ascending Christology starts with the man Jesus of Nazareth, and, looking at his beautiful life, asks about his relationship to God, or about how God is present in him.

This raises another difficulty with a descending Christology. Such a Christology suggests that God suddenly visits earth from outside, and then, after a brief stay, departs again for heaven. Is there no abiding presence of God in the world before or after the career of Jesus? If there is, and it seems there is an abiding presence and manifestation of God in all creation, might it not be a more adequate Christological model to look for an especially intense and powerful presence of God in Jesus?

5. **Chalcedon says little or nothing about salvation.** This is a serious limitation. Chalcedon concentrates entirely on the constitution of Jesus and says nothing about what difference he makes to human life. This leaves it very impoverished, and is perhaps one of the main reasons why Christology since has been so impoverished, confining itself mainly to the question of Jesus' ontological makeup, a question the New Testament is content to leave quite open. Granted the importance of the matter, one could agree fully with Chalcedon's handling of it and be a poor Christian, or hold a rather different view of Je-

sus' composition and be an outstanding Christian. Chalcedon's definitions are anything but an exhaustive treatment of Christology, and may even be focused on the less important issues. Many Christians lived and died as disciples of Jesus in the four hundred years before Chalcedon, and experienced God's love and salvation in him, without the Council's philosophical answer to the question of his identity.

These are some of the main objections brought against the Christological definition of the Council of Chalcedon. They are part of the motivation for contemporary efforts to reformulate our Christological faith. Neither the criticisms of a previous formulation nor the attempt to reformulate represents a loss of faith or a disrespect for tradition. Those who reformulate are themselves disciples of Jesus, the vast majority of them pastors in daily contact with people's questions and difficulties. In the hands of such people as these, reformulation is always an attempt to preserve the heart of the faith as the tradition presents it, but to put it in contemporary thought forms and language, so that people today can find it more fully intelligible and credible. Let us move then to a consideration of the main accents of the contemporary reformulation.

QUESTIONS FOR DISCUSSION

1. What is the importance of the Council of Chalcedon for Christology? What did the Council define?
2. What are some of the criticisms that theologians today bring against Chalcedon? What is your evaluation of these criticisms?
3. What is your assessment of Chalcedon and its Christology?
4. Why reformulate Christology when it has already been formulated?

IV. The Contemporary Reformulation

Our procedure in this chapter will be to move through several important theologians of the present century, calling attention to the highlights of their presentation of Jesus. These thinkers are drawn from several Christian denominations. Even all together, they do not represent the whole of contemporary Christology, but they do give us a good idea of its characteristic thrust. Through all the variations of their individual presentations of the matter, there emerges a fairly clear consensus, an interpretation of Jesus which avoids most of the problems of Chalcedon while protecting what Chalcedon was trying to protect. Let us look at the work of Karl Rahner, some representatives of process thought (Norman Pittenger, John Cobb, Jr., David Griffin), Paul Tillich, D.M. Baillie, Edward Schillebeeckx, and Piet Schoonenberg.

KARL RAHNER

Perhaps the most accessible framework for understanding how contemporary theology views Jesus is that of Karl Rahner. A German Roman Catholic, Rahner has probably been the best known and most influential theologian in Roman Catholic circles over the last forty years. His output is prodigious, and it always gives evidence of a deep knowledge of and respect for the tradition combined with a desire to find the heart of the faith and put it in contemporary language. To enter into Rahner's thought world, we must first look at his descriptions of the human person and of God.

Rahner characterizes the human person as the mystery of infinite emptiness. He never tires of saying that we are a mystery to ourselves. All through our lives, we are trying to figure ourselves out—who we are, why we do what we do, what our life is all about, and what we want. Though our understanding grows as we live along, we never get to the bottom of the mystery. We remain ever a question to ourselves. And emptiness is a large part of the mystery. We get in touch with it in quietness, when we turn the TV and stereo off, and do not pick up the phone or go out, or pour ourselves a drink or take up another task. We are empty, and the emptiness frightens us. Sometimes it comes on us unawares, in the midst of the party, in the mall of the shopping center, in bed in the middle of the night. Our emptiness is a hunger, crying out to be filled with something, we know not quite what. It is a cry for meaning, for companionship, for fulfillment. What shows the hunger to be infinite is that although we can find something of the things we long for, we can never seem to find enough.

Rahner characterizes God as the mystery of infinite fullness. God is utterly beyond our comprehension. How God creates is beyond our ken. What God may be doing in the world eludes us. Whatever it is, God's ways are clearly not ours. The God we deal with in our prayer seems often to be distant and indifferent. One of Rahner's books on prayer is called *Encounters with Silence*, a not particularly hopeful title. Our theological dogmas are no more exempt from this struggle with mystery. They falter in their attempts to articulate what we believe, and fall short of the mystery no matter how carefully or authoritatively we formulate them. Even when we shall have come to enjoy the beatific vision, seeing God, as it were, face to face, the mystery will not be removed but will continue to fascinate us and provoke wonder. Rahner does not develop the notions of infinite or fullness, but both are traditional descriptions of God.

As can be seen, Rahner's notions of the human person and of God are correlative. This is not surprising, since our notion of God is derived from our experience of God, and we can experience God only in relation to ourselves, not independently. In relation to ourselves, God is the mysterious source of the world and of ourselves, and that mystery of infinite fullness for which we long. Rahner's favorite metaphor for God is that God is the horizon of all our experiencing. It is in the nature of a horizon not to be directly seen, but to be the background against which everything else is seen. The metaphor thus expresses how God is at least dimly in our awareness, always at the edges of consciousness, yet not yet in our possession as that fullness for which we long.

There is a dynamism at both ends of the relationship. On the side of the human person, it is a restless yearning, which Rahner calls the transcendence of the human spirit. We see the limitation of every answer we receive to our questions, and we strain toward a fuller answer. We see the limitedness of every good we lay hold of, and strain toward a more satisfying good. There is also a dynamism on the side of God. God is self-revealing and extends toward us for a relationship. God does not remain self-enclosed but reaches out toward all persons to be their fulfillment. Of God's self-communication we are at least in some measure aware. We know both the comfort of God and the challenge of God as they touch our lives. Sometimes we accept them, and sometimes we resist.

Now we are in a position to understand how Rahner views Jesus. Jesus is that person in whom the mystery of infinite emptiness and the mystery of infinite fullness come together perfectly. God fills him, and he allows himself to be filled so totally that he and God become functionally one. His life is completely taken over by God, absolutely given to God, so that he can say, in the words of the Fourth Gospel, "The Father and I are one" (Jn 10:31). In fact, the Fourth Gospel contains many statements which describe different aspects of this functional identity between Jesus and God in word and work.

He who sees me sees the Father (Jn 14:9).

I do always the things that are pleasing to him (Jn 8:29).

I do nothing of myself, but just as the Father has taught me, I speak these things (Jn 8:28).

If I am not doing the works of my Father, do not believe me. But if I am doing them, even though you do not believe me, believe the works, in order that you may come to know and may continue knowing that the Father is in me and I in the Father (Jn 10:37).

The Son cannot do anything of himself, but only what he sees the Father doing. For whatever things that one does, these things the Son also does in like manner (Jn 5:19).

All of these statements reflect that perfect union in love and operation that obtains between Jesus and God. It is as if he is saying that he has no life of his own and desires none except to be completely at God's disposal, to speak the words of God and do the deeds of God. There is an echo of this later in Paul, who says of his own life, "I live, now not I, but Christ lives in me" (Gal 2:20). That is the kind of complete takeover envisioned in Rahner's Christology.

In this Christology, Jesus is on a plane with us. He does not descend from heaven. God is very much present and active in him, and in this sense it is a "descending" Christology.

But Jesus is a human person as we are human persons, and he has a relationship to God as we have a relationship to God. What makes him unique is that his relationship to God is ever so much more full. He is the fulfillment of what all of us in our deepest selfhood want to be. Indeed he reveals to us what we are called to be, what the highest human possibility is. He is our brother, and yet miles ahead of us. Every person is a possible self-revelation of God, and in some degree an actual self-revelation of God. This is what we mean when we say to someone, "I find God in you," or "God speaks to me in you." We are especially aware of the presence of God in certain persons; they are carriers of an unmistakable spiritual power, which strikes us in their words and bearing. What every person is, at least by vocation, Jesus is in the highest possible actuality. Thus he is the revelation of what the human person is, and of who God is for us, as both are seen in him.

PROCESS THEOLOGY

Process theology uses somewhat different language, but it develops essentially the same conception. Norman Pittenger, a Protestant theologian who has published voluminously on Christian topics from within a deep Christian faith, objects to the presentation of Jesus as a sort of "divine intruder." If Jesus is so interpreted, he says, then Jesus is not only not really human, but the implication is that God is not usually in the world. The process conception of God is that God is creative love, present in the world and in each entity in the world always. God is not just present to everything, but active in everything, drawing the world and each entity within it by the power of the divine attraction to the ends God intends for each and for the whole. God informs every level of being, present and active in widely differing degrees of intensity and significance. Jesus both manifests and imparts the divine activity in a uniquely full manner. In him, God was united with a human life to as full an extent as it is to us conceivable that a genuine human life can receive and assimilate God. Thus Jesus is the revelation of God in terms of humanity, God revealed insofar as a human person is capable of revealing God. God's self-revelation is never just a showing, but is also action and operation, as in the great deeds of God on behalf of the Hebrews in the Hebrew Scriptures. In Jesus, God releases into the world a new stream of divine energy for the regeneration of all creation.

Two other Protestant theologians in the process tradition, John Cobb, Jr. and David Griffin, put these same ideas in slightly different terms. Jesus helps us understand God's working in the world as creative love everywhere immanently present. Jesus embodies that love in the highest degree, and not only shows it but furthers its working. A whole "field of force" is generated by his life, death, and resurrection, and this field of force is ever after embedded in the world's history, because every event lives on in succeeding events by its influence. The Jesus event is a powerful one, further strengthened by remembrance and re-enactment. Whatever comes within a field of force is moved to conform to some measure. And so it is with Jesus and his influence. It becomes a transforming power in history, the supreme expression of God's creative love.

To describe Jesus' relationship to God still more precisely, Cobb and Griffin start with the premise that Jesus is fully human. The presence of God in him is not an exception to the general way God is present (or incarnate) in all things and especially in human beings. The difference is that in Jesus, this incarnation of God constitutes Jesus' very selfhood. That is, Jesus' life purposes and God's purpose for him are one and the same. Jesus' whole intent is to do the will of the Father, to be available for the Father's work. Jesus and God remain distinct in being, but functionally they become one by reason of the divine indwelling and the extent to which Jesus opens himself and conforms to it. Thus who God is and what God is doing on behalf of humankind becomes evident in Jesus. Particularly evident in Jesus is the way God's creative love works in the world. It never forces. It only lures, attracts, persuades.

PAUL TILLICH

We find similar Christological accents in the theology of Paul Tillich, the German-born Protestant theologian who did so much of his work in the United States. Tillich operates in a different philosophical framework than process thinkers do. But his reading of Jesus is very similar to what we have already seen.

Whereas the rest of humankind is in a fallen state of estrangement or alienation from God, whom Tillich names the Ground of all Being, Jesus is perfectly united with God. And Jesus maintains this unity through all the trials of his difficult mission, in the face of all his temptations, so that God and salvation are always seen in him. Jesus is not the only revelation of God. There is a revelation of God in all created things, and there are special ecstatic manifestations of the Ground of Being in certain events, persons, and things. Jesus is the full and decisive manifestation; all others are partial. Jesus is therefore the criterion by which all others are to be judged.

For Tillich, it is the being of Jesus that is decisive rather than Jesus' teaching, works, or death and resurrection. These latter are just expressions of a totality, which is the entire being of Jesus as an embodiment of what Tillich calls "the New Being." What Tillich means by New Being is the power in Jesus to conquer existential estrangement. Jesus conquers it himself, and gives all others the power to overcome it in their own lives. Jesus maintains unbroken unity with God. He surrenders his whole life to being the Christ, i.e., letting God be manifested in him.

Tillich does not like the term "incarnation" understood in its ordinary sense. Nor does he like the formulation "God became man," because it suggests that God was transmuted into a human being. He rejects the notion of two natures in one person, because he does not think that the term "nature" applies to God. Tillich has a profound respect for the transcendence or mystery of God. A human person cannot *be* God. Nothing in the world can be anything more than a symbol for God, though a symbol does participate in that Ground of Being which it expresses. This is the way Tillich views Jesus, as the fullest expression in human terms of God, who is the ground and source of all being. Tillich thinks it is clearer and more accurate to avoid some of the traditional verbal formulations, and to speak instead of a dynamic relation between the man Jesus and God. He refers to the paradox of Jesus Christ as "eternal God-man unity."

D.M. BAILLIE

The Anglican theologian D.M. Baillie calls his book on Christology *God Was in Christ*. The phrase, which comes from 2 Corinthians 5:19, perfectly expresses Baillie's Christological position. To develop his Christology, Baillie begins with the central Christian paradox, that of grace. The paradox of grace is all the good Christians do is somehow done not by them but by God, without abrogating human personality or removing personal responsibility. The paradox is well expressed by Paul in a personal way when he says:

> By God's grace I am what I am, and God's grace toward me has not been in vain, but I have labored more than all of them (the Apostles). Yet not I, but the grace of God in me (1 Cor 15:10).

We are never more ourselves, never more truly free, than in those moments of which we can say it was all God's doing. This kind of working together of the divine and human becomes for Baillie the key to understanding the incarnation of God in Jesus of Nazareth. Jesus claimed no glory for himself, but ascribed it all to God. Because he was so completely surrendered to God in love and obedience, God could fully accomplish the divine purpose through him, manifesting self in Jesus and working through him for the salvation of humankind. What we see in the saints, Baillie is saying, we find preeminently in Jesus, whose life is totally shaped by God and so has on us an impact of tremendous spiritual power.

There are other aspects of Baillie's Christology, but this is the central notion, this explication of Jesus in terms of the working of God's grace. As can be seen, the model is very similar to those already reviewed.

EDWARD SCHILLEBEECKX

Edward Schillebeeckx, the Dutch Roman Catholic theologian whose two lengthy volumes *Jesus* and *Christ* are probably the most exhaustive labor of exegesis and systematic theological reflection in the field to date, sees Jesus' "Abba experience" as the source and secret of Jesus' being, message, and manner of life. Schillebeeckx notes that Jesus' use of the term "Abba" for God is unique to him and is present in the earliest strata of the Gospel tradition, which shows that the usage is really Jesus' own rather than an attribution of later theological reflection. The term's closest equivalents in English are "daddy" or "papa." It was a name commonly enough used by children for their fathers in Jewish families in Jesus' time, but never before applied to God. That Jesus applied the name to God indicates the intense intimacy and familiarity of his relationship with God. Schillebeeckx calls it the heart of Jesus' religious experience, the grounding of his conviction that he was in some special way God's Son. It was the ground not only of his being, but of his message and manner of life as well. Jesus' deep religious rapport with God was the basis of his conviction that God is bent upon the good of humanity, which became the inspiration of his whole ministry of healing and reconciliation as well as of his call to trust in God. Thus Schillebeeckx, too, focuses on the uniquely intimate relationship between the man Jesus and the transcendent God. There are no ghosts or gods in disguise wandering around in our human history, Schillebeeckx says, only humans. Yet this particular human, Jesus of Nazareth, succeeded in touching off a religious movement that became a world religion asserting that Jesus is the revelation, in personal form, of God. For Schillebeeckx, the explanation of that fact lies in people's experience of God's presence and saving power in him. This is why Schillebeeckx spends most of his pages exploring the question of how Jesus brings salvation rather than the question of Jesus' identity. He notes that Jesus himself was not concerned about his identity but only about his function: what he was supposed to say and do in God's name. Those passages of Scripture which focus on who he is show a later interpretive hand.

On the question of Jesus' identity, Schillebeeckx' conceptualization is very similar to that of the other theologians so far
examined in this chapter. He holds that if God somehow appears in Jesus, it will be within Jesus' humanity. God and a human person do not exist side by side as commensurate
quantities but rather the one within the other, i.e., God is im-
manent within the person while yet transcending the person.
Thus God is partly revealed, partly veiled in Jesus just because
of the disproportion between God and a human being.

When Schillebeeckx summarizes his detailed study of the
Fourth Gospel, the Gospel which more than any other New
Testament document was the basis of Chalcedonian Christology, he observes that John puts forward a functional rather
than an ontological Christology, i.e., one concerned with what
Jesus does rather than with who he is. John views the relation-
ship between Jesus and God in functional terms. For John, Jesus is really a man, but a man in a unique, all-surpassing
relationship with God. The Father, whom Jesus familiarly calls
Abba, and Jesus are two persons, but they are one in love and
will and work. Thus Jesus reveals God by revealing himself.
The Father remains the greater (Jn 14:28), the one whose will
Jesus is concerned to do (Jn 4:34; 5:19; 8:29), the entire goal of
Jesus' career (Jn 13:1; 14:12; 16:10; 17:11; 20:17). In Jesus, God
has come to us, and God is revealed as a God of human beings:
"God is love" (1 Jn 4:8).

PIET SCHOONENBERG

Piet Schoonenberg is, like Schillebeeckx, a Dutch Roman
Catholic theologian, extensively published and well known for
his contributions to theology. We find in his Christology much

the same thrust we find in the others we have seen. He articulates many of the objections against the Chalcedonian pattern that we reviewed in the last chapter. Because of these difficulties, he proposes that we reformulate in these terms: Instead of saying "Jesus, God and man," let us say "Jesus, God in man." This verbal reformulation is Schoonenberg's distinctive contribution. He is convinced that we can make this change and still be faithful to the original faith-insight of Chalcedon, while shedding the problems entailed in the conciliar pronouncement.

Schoonenberg's starting points are two: (1) Jesus is one person; (2) Jesus is a human person. Both points are clear in the New Testament, and beyond dispute in the tradition of the Church. There is no question in the Gospels of Jesus being a split personality, of his acting now out of his humanity, now out of his divinity. There is no question in the Gospels of Jesus praying to himself, the human to the divine, or of any other type of divine/human dialogue within himself. He prays to someone distinct from himself, whom he calls Father. It is his name for God. Jesus is one person. And he is a human person. No one in his public life calls this human personhood of his into question, nor, for that matter, do any of the New Testament writers, even in the light of the resurrection. In the very early strata of the Gospels we find the popular puzzlement over his extraordinary powers, a puzzlement based in the conviction that he is one with all of them.

> "Where did he get all this? What kind of wisdom is he endowed with? How is it that such miraculous deeds are accomplished by his hands? Is this not the carpenter, the son of Mary, a brother of James and Joses and Judas and Simon? Are not his sisters our neighbors here?" They found him too much for them (Mk 6:2–3).

It is precisely because Jesus is taken unquestioningly as a human person that his authoritative teaching, even what is called his "making himself equal to God" (Jn 5:18), is looked upon as so alarming, so "blasphemous."

Now when Schoonenberg establishes this second premise, that Jesus is a human person, he is already reformulating the Chalcedonian Christology, in which, as we saw, Jesus is viewed as having a human nature, but not as being a human person. In the traditional formulation, the personal center of Jesus is that of the second person of the Blessed Trinity, who has assumed a human nature. So this is a very significant shift. God is now understood to be present in a human person, rather than that a human nature subsists in a divine person. But how is God present in Jesus? In the same basic way that God is present in anything else, i.e., in such a way as to be the source of its being and to be self-expressive through it, but without violating or in any way interfering with the way the created thing is in its own nature. Thus Jesus is truly and perfectly a man, just a "common" man like everyone else, but with God expressed through his humanity in a most extraordinary degree. Schoonenberg calls his Christology "the theory of the presence of God through his Word in Jesus Christ."

Schoonenberg calls Jesus the "eschatological" person, i.e., the highest realization of humanity. He is not essentially different from us, yet, precisely as a man, he spoke as no one else has ever spoken, and did things that no one else has ever done. His relationship to God is superior to ours. It is clear and immediate, and he can speak for God with authority. His relationship to other human beings is superior too. His love is universal and generously self-sacrificing. He is the dynamic embodiment of God's boundless love for every person, however negligible or lost that person might appear to be.

THE CONTEMPORARY REFORMULATION
AND SCRIPTURE

Is there any scriptural basis for a reformulation in terms of Jesus "God in man" rather than "God and man"? Investigation shows that there is. The New Testament quite commonly speaks the basic language of this formulation. By contrast, we have already seen how sparingly the New Testament calls Jesus "God." Let us look at some of the passages where God is said to be *in* Jesus.

The Father is in me, and I am in the Father (Jn 10:38).

Do you not believe that I am in the Father and the Father in me? (Jn 14:10).

I pray also for those who will believe in me through their word, that all may be one as you, Father, are in me, and I in you; I pray that they may be (one) in us, that the world may believe that you sent me (Jn 17:20–21).

God was in Christ, reconciling the world to himself, not counting men's offenses against them (2 Cor 5:19).

In him (Christ) dwells all the fullness of the divinity bodily (Col 2:9).

God, who long ago spoke on many occasions and in many ways to our forefathers in the prophets, has at the end of these days spoken to us in a son (Heb 1:1).

Thus the contemporary formulation is by no means a new one. It goes back to the New Testament itself.

In fact, the New Testament, in some of its earlier strata, presents us with a Jesus whose relationship with God is put in the even less specific terms that God is *with* him or acting *through* him. Looking at the following passages from the earliest post-resurrection preaching in Acts, we can see how clear it is that Jesus is regarded as a man, yet one uniquely empowered by God and finally glorified by God.

> People of Israel, listen to me! Jesus of Nazareth was a man whom God sent to you with miracles, wonders, and signs as his credentials. These God worked through him in your midst, as you well know. He was delivered up by the set plan and purpose of God; you even made use of pagans to crucify and kill him. God freed him from death's bitter pangs, however, and raised him up again, for it was impossible that death should keep its hold on him . . . . Therefore let the whole house of Israel know beyond any doubt that God has made both Lord and Messiah this Jesus whom you crucified (Acts 2:22–24, 36).

> I take it you all know what has been reported all over Judea about Jesus of Nazareth, beginning in Galilee with the baptism John preached; of the way God anointed him with the Holy Spirit and power. He went about doing good works and healing all who were in the grip of the devil, because God was with him (Acts 10:37–38; see also Acts 3:13–15; 4:9–12; 5:29–32).

We had occasion to observe earlier that not just one but many Christologies exist in the New Testament. These passages show us the so called "low" Christology of early Christian preaching. It was the "high" Christology of John that was principally reflected in the Chalcedonian formula. But the passages we saw just above from John show that even there the "God in Christ" formula is common enough. And as Schillebeeckx points out, even in the Johannine passages which identify Jesus and God as one, it is a functional identity that is being articulated. Jesus and God are one not in being, but in love and will and work.

The thrust of contemporary theology is to allow Jesus a full and genuine humanity, in accordance with both Scripture and tradition, and to preserve the Christian faith confession of Jesus' divinity. It is also concerned to remove elements in our faith confession which might be an unnecessary stumbling block to faith. And it endeavors to accomplish its task in concepts and language consonant with the contemporary experience of reality. At the risk of oversimplification, it seems to be the basic thrust of contemporary theology to change the Chalcedonian formula "Jesus, God and man" to the formula "Jesus, God in man."

The reformulation naturally gives rise to some questions. We will examine some of them shortly. But first, in order to grasp more fully what has been said in this chapter in the abstract, conceptual language of the left brain, it might be helpful to put the same ideas in the concrete, intuitive, story-form of the right brain. This we will attempt in the next chapter. Then we will take up the questions.

QUESTIONS FOR DISCUSSION

1. How would you state the contemporary reformulation?
2. Is this reformulation faithful to Church tradition?
3. Is there any basis in Scripture for the contemporary presentation of Christ?

V. The Inner Experience of Jesus

In the present state of New Testament scholarship, it is impossible to reconstruct the life of Jesus in its details with any certitude. We will go into the reasons for this more fully in the next chapter. For the present, suffice it to say that there is an historical bedrock in the Gospel materials. But there is such an adaptation of the history in the interest of expressing mature, post-resurrection faith that it is difficult to separate out the solidly historical substratum. The Gospel writers are mainly concerned to tell who Jesus Christ, risen and living in the Church, is for our life of faith now. They do it on the basis of incidents from his public ministry, adapted for their purposes. If they are not careful to preserve exact sequences and historical details, still less are they apparently interested in describing for us what was going on inside Jesus. These are the reasons why the reconstruction of the historical career of Jesus in this chapter, including some attention to his inner experience, can only be hypothetical. Yet all who have believed in Jesus and loved him have longed to know him as fully as possible, and it would be not only impossible but positively counterproductive to try to block our imaginations from venturing into this terrain, guided by what bits of information and hints we possess. The present chapter is an attempt to do that in the light of the contemporary reformulation we have just studied. If Jesus is really a human person whose experience is like ours in most respects except that his relationship to God goes well beyond ours in its degree, what might his life experience have been like?

He is born into a religious family. At an early age he learns from his mother and father the great traditions about Yahweh, the God who saves from trouble, the God who gives the law, the God who is faithful to the people in spite of their sinfulness. His parents teach him to pray, and introduce him to the religious rituals which have come down from their ancestors. His home is peaceful, his childhood memories happy.

From early on he notices in himself a strong attraction to prayer. He loves the rituals and festivals of his time. Even more, he loves to go off by himself to pray. He finds deep peace and contentment in the presence of God. He feels loved, and he loves. He does not think of this as in any way special. He has nothing to compare it with.

One childhood memory that stands out for him is the religious festival in Jerusalem during his early adolescence (Lk 2:41–52). Filled by this time with religious questions, he strikes up a conversation with one of the rabbis. Before they have talked very long, the rabbi calls over a friend of his: "Come here. I want you to meet a most unusual boy. His religious insight is extraordinary." Before the conversation is over, he is talking with four of the rabbis, and forgets all about his parents. From that day, he begins thinking seriously about becoming a rabbi or priest. He has already received, and continues to receive, much encouragement.

His father breaks him into the carpenter's trade, and Jesus learns the art of making things with his hands and dealing with the villagers. He likes the quiet and simplicity of the daily routine most of the time. Other days he feels a restlessness and his thoughts wander far from the shop. He becomes a keen observer of the human scene. He feels compassion for human suffering, and puzzles over the problem of evil. His prayer life continues, deep and strong.

In his twenties, he begins to have serious doubts about the religion of his time. It seems so complex, so legalistic, so rigid. Its leaders strike him as functionaries, going through the motions, living and teaching an external observance of law and ritual which fails to engage the heart or impart any spiritual power. It becomes increasingly difficult for Jesus to find anything of value in the weekly synagogue service. He feels as if he is losing his faith, and the prospect frightens him. His contact with God in prayer is also troubled. He reaches out for help, and finds very little. The priests and rabbis are uncomfortable with his questions, and counsel him to set them aside and just believe. No one can help him much with his struggle over how to think of God. The crisis deepens, and so does his loneliness.

About this time a man by the name of John becomes prominent, preaching a baptism of repentance (Lk 3:1–22). Jesus goes out to hear him and is impressed with what he hears. John strikes him as a man of God, and his baptism makes sense as a sign of one's desire to turn one's life completely over to God. Jesus decides to be baptized. As he prays after being baptized, he has the most extraordinary religious experience of his life. He hears the words "Beloved Son" and "My Servant" whispered to him over and over in his deepest consciousness. It is as if God is speaking directly and unmistakably to him personally, with words of tenderest love and with an intimation of some special destiny. His own response, which feels as if it is given to him, is "Abba," a term more intimate than "Father," which ever after that day is at the heart of his prayer. He feels rejoined at a profound level to the God he thought he was losing. And the Spirit of God fills his being.

After this experience, he begins discussing his religious ideas with his friends. Some are threatened. Some respond very positively. The latter bring others to him: "You've got to meet Jesus. He's a remarkable person, and he has some amazing ideas." As the circle grows, Jesus is invited one sabbath to preach in the synagogue. His audience listens intently. But in

the aftermath, he learns that he has caused quite a ruckus.
There are those who are enthusiastically supportive. But there
are others who do not like what they hear, who question his
credentials and make it plain that they do not want to hear him
again. Jesus is struck by their closed-mindedness, and learns
something about politics in religion.

About this time he has another remarkable experience.
He is in the synagogue one sabbath and he sees a spastic man.
His heart goes out to him, and he feels moved to speak to him.
In the course of the conversation, he asks the man if it is all
right if he lays his hands on him and prays for him. The man
assents, and Jesus does so. As Jesus prays for him, the man
gradually becomes still, and then says he feels completely different. Jesus is astonished. The results far exceed anything he
had hoped for. He has discovered another gift. It is the beginning of his ministry of healing.

Now the carpenter is caught in a conflict. His notoriety is
growing and his life is increasingly taken up with people's demands. Wherever he goes, people are prevailing on him either
to teach them or to lay hands on them and pray. He does not
like the public forum. He much prefers the quiet life. Particularly disturbing to him is the social conflict to which his words
and deeds seem always to give rise. But his compassion for human suffering runs deep, and he knows he has special gifts. He
prays the conflict through, and decides he must continue his
public ministry. He cannot stop teaching what he believes. He
feels confirmed in it both by his prayer and by the responses
of many people. And he cannot withhold his gift of healing. So
he goes on with his work, bearing its pains.

His ministry attracts women (Lk 7:36–51; 8:1–3; 10:38–
42). They love to listen to him and be with him. And he enjoys
talking with them. Often theirs is the most sensitive religious
understanding, and from them he feels a response, an acceptance, and a love that are deeply moving. Friendships develop,

some of them to last a lifetime, and out of them one particularly strong love. Jesus considers marriage. He feels a powerful attraction toward it, buttressed by a cultural expectation that everyone eventually marries and has a family. But as he prays it through, it does not feel quite right to him, does not seem to be his call. His ministry has become so all-absorbing that he does not see how he could give himself to wife and family in the way they deserve (Mk 2:13; 3:7–12; 3:20). He is also convinced that the end time is near (Mk 9:1). Besides, he has already aroused public opposition to a point that seems ominous, which at the very least would mean ongoing suffering for his wife and family. He decides, with difficulty, to forego marriage.

One day he is taking a break with his close friends, away from the constant crowd (Mk 6:30–32; 8:27–29). It has been a day of fishing and picnicking and talking things over. The feeling in the group is close, the moment right, and Jesus decides to unburden himself.

> I need your help with something. I'm not sure I like the way things are going for me. Sometimes I feel as if I am losing my mind. I got my start in a small town, in a little family business, and I loved the simplicity of it. I have no special education. And here I find myself in the midst of a religious storm, the center of public controversy. Some of my relatives think I'm crazy (Mk 3:20–21). Other people say I'm possessed. I do love God and I do love people. But I never asked for this, and often I wonder what to do about it. I have this vision of myself going off to the desert to join the Essene community. Maybe I'm just stirring up trouble here. I'd like to get away from it all, and live out the rest of my life in quietness and contemplation. Yet I feel pulled by the immense needs of people. And sometimes I feel like Jeremiah, with the word of God burning inside me

(Jer 15:10–21; 20:7–9). You are my closest friends, and know me best. What do you think?

The group draws closer, and different individuals begin to speak.

Look at what you're doing. The blind see, the lame walk, and the poor are comforted by good news. Isaiah says those are the things God's holy one will do (Is 35:4–6). You certainly cannot be doing things like that and not be in union with God.

You should hear people talk about you. Sure, some are against you, and they make no secret of the fact, especially the authorities. They're threatened by you and the things you stand for. Some are just plain jealous of your popularity and power. But they cannot ignore you. And some of them have converted and joined us. Most people are tremendously helped by all you are doing.

I watch you eat and drink with the outcasts, which is a pretty telling bit of testimony in itself, and then I listen to them talk. They say they experience God in you as they never have in anyone else. It's your acceptance of them, your reverence for them, and the power of the simple stories you share with them. They've long since given up on religion, but they find in you a God they can believe in.

This may sound strange, but when I'm with you I feel as if I am with God. I've never said that to anyone else. There is a peace, a love, and a healing power in you that I have never encountered anywhere. You've completely changed my life.

Jesus is moved by these confirmations, coming to him with such unmistakable consensus from the group. Something deep inside him resonates with them, even as he is surprised to hear what is being said. He feels moved to share with them some of his very personal religious experiences, and this leads to an even stronger confirmation from them. They tell him they see him as one specially anointed by God to be a prophet, healer, and teacher, as somehow God's own saving outreach to people of every kind. They encourage him to continue what he is doing, in spite of the cost.

It is not long after this that Jesus has his great experience on the mountain (Lk 9:28–36). As he prays, he has an intense awareness of God's presence within him. It is as if his whole being is suffused with light, and the feelings that go with it nearly overpower him. Again he hears those words from his baptism, "My Son!" "My Beloved!" whispered to him over and over, and he feels the most profound union with God. And again he has a premonition of some great trial to come. The experience amazes and overwhelms him. It confirms him still more deeply in everything he is about. He knows for certain now that he speaks and acts with God's authority and approval. And so he continues his work, and his following grows.

The opposition is getting ugly now. In every crowd there are critics and spies who make it increasingly difficult for him (Mt 21:23–27; 45–46; Lk 11:53–54). He is misrepresented. His way is blocked. His work is undermined. He is threatened with imprisonment, with death (Jn 7:32; 8:59; 10:31). Even the Romans are watching him. Some well intentioned friends urge him to join the zealot movement and help throw off the Roman yoke through armed struggle. They tell him that he could be king of a reformed religious state which would really serve God as God should be served. The idea has some plausibility, and he prays about it. But it does not feel right, and his choice remains constant to be the defenseless prophet, the suffering servant. He confides to his friends that he expects to be killed. He does not know when it will strike or how, whether he will be suddenly stabbed in the crowd, or kidnaped and disposed of secretly, or possibly even arrested and crucified, the fate of political agitators. He lives now knowing that any day might be his last, and he prepares himself and his friends for it, even as he pours himself the more earnestly into his ministry.

As he feels the net of death closing inexorably around him, Jesus is stricken with a profound sadness. He loves life, and it grieves him to think he must lose it. He loves his solitary walks in the hills (Jn 6:15; Mk 1:45). He loves the fishing trips with his friends, the picnics, the camping out under the stars. He loves all things natural (Mt 13). The beauty of children touches him especially. He loves to play with them and ask them questions (Mk 10:13–16). He cherishes his contacts with the outcasts of society, people whose goodness is hidden from themselves, but who seem to find it again as he eats and drinks and talks with them. For that matter, he loves his whole ministry, even with its difficulties. He feels driven to extend himself yet further, that more people might enjoy a better life (Mk 1:37–38; Jn 10:10). He feels as if his work is just begun, yet his time is very limited now. He will have to say goodbye soon to many dear people, to a couple of very special women, to Lazarus, his mother, and the Twelve. There seems to be no way he can avoid this death, unless he flees, or falls silent, or changes his tune, none of which he can in conscience do.

In his prayer he gradually begins to see other possibilities in this impending death of his. Perhaps it could be a gift. It could be a way of saying that he believed unshakably and to the end in what he had taught (Jn 17:7–8; 17:14). It could be a way of witnessing to his trust in God in spite of all the tragic and dreadful things that happen in this world (Jn 16:33). In the way he faced death, he could give evidence of his conviction that there was life beyond the horizons of this world (Jn 14:1–4). In the way he bore suffering and death, he could be a support to all those who suffer, who struggle to endure it with dignity and find some meaning in it. Gradually his death takes on quite a different aspect in his thinking, and he begins to see it as a positive opportunity to express the love he bears toward God and all human beings (Jn 14:30–31; Mk 10:45; Jn 13:1). He understands it indeed as something his Father is asking of him. And he begins to tell his friends that he actually wants to die, to lay down his life for his friends (Lk 12:50; Jn 10:11–18).

He is informed that the plot has been fully laid, that the next night they are planning to arrest him and bring him to trial. He has little doubt what the outcome will be. His deepest wish is to have a final meal with his friends, and he asks them to make the arrangements (Lk 22:7–13). All through that day he puzzles over what he might leave them as a remembrance. He does not possess very much, and nothing he possesses seems to speak what he wants to say to them. Finally it comes to him. He will say what he wants to say to them with bread and wine, and leave them that.

He gathers with them for a final meal. It is a celebration resting on a great sadness (Lk 22:14–16). They talk about the good times and about the love that has grown among them for one another. They talk about what is happening around them, and what is going to come to him. He shares with them his final thoughts (Jn 13–17). Tenderly he washes the feet of each one, expressing his love (Jn 13:1–17). Then he takes the bread and wine and identifies himself with them (Mt 26:26–29), identifies himself with the bread broken and passed around for the sustaining of life, and with the wine of fellowship and celebration. These things best say all that he has meant and would mean on the morrow, and would stand as an everlasting memorial of him. And so they conclude their meal (Mt 26:30).

And then in no time he is swept into his passion. It is one thing to talk about suffering and death, he discovers, another to go through them. It is far worse than he has anticipated. He witnesses the pervasive corruption of a whole political and religious system. He sees loyal friends desert him (Mk 14:50; 66–72). He experiences the wanton cruelty of professional torturers and executioners (Mk 15:15–20). He wonders whether God really is in charge in the world, or whether the power of evil holds sway. His suffering is terrible. He doubts himself, wondering whether he perhaps has had illusions of grandeur and is, after all, the public nuisance they make him out to be, a troublemaker and a blasphemer—or, more terrifying still, a dreamer. The worst part of it is that God now seems so far far away, so utterly indifferent in this his hour of greatest need. He cries out in his agony (Mk 15:33–34).

The darkness of death deepens. It is all but over now. As he feels the last breath of life slipping from his pain-racked body, he glimpses a dim light at the end of his long tunnel of darkness. And he walks step by step toward and into the embrace of his Father, and feels himself transformed into a being of radiance. Now he perceives clearly how God has always been with him and in him and operating through him, even in these last dreadful hours. Now he knows how specially he has been loved, yet how delicately God has respected his freedom and awaited his cooperation in everything. Now he knows clearly for the first time the permanent significance of his life, death, and resurrection, and realizes that he can be present in a new way to people of every time and place. Now as God crowns him with love and honor and glory, he understands how extraordinary his gifts truly are and how preeminent his achievement by God's grace. The crucified one has been made the exalted one, Lord and Christ forever.

QUESTIONS FOR DISCUSSION

1. What limits our ability to reconstruct the events of Jesus' outer or inner life with much certitude?

2. What usefulness, if any, is there in trying to reconstruct the story?
3. How does the narrative presented in this chapter change the way you think about Jesus? What sorts of questions does it raise for you?
4. How would you tell the story?

VI. Common Questions

In this chapter we will address some of the questions which typically arise when contemporary Christology is discussed. Among them are: (1) How can anyone change the formula of an ecumenical council? (2) What does the *Church* teach about Christology today? (3) In the perspective of contemporary Christology, is there any reason why the phenomenon of Jesus cannot occur again in another time and place? (4) If the story told in the last chapter about Jesus' inner experience is true, why don't we find it in the Gospels? (5) How does the contemporary reformulation affect my relationship to Jesus? In the next chapter we will treat two further questions which require some elaboration: What does contemporary Christology say about Jesus' pre-existence, and what does it say about the Trinity?

As we begin, let us say a word to put contemporary Christology in perspective. Probably most of us were raised within just one Christological view, that of Chalcedon, coming to us through catechism or Sunday school. It feels jarring to hear a different one, and it arouses some fear. Here it may be helpful to remember that there are a plurality of Christologies in the New Testament itself, and that this plurality is part of the New Testament's richness. The early Christian communities believed somewhat differently from one another, though all put faith in Jesus. Then over the centuries there were further developments in the articulation of Christian faith. Chalcedon was one of these, in Greek philosophical categories, and it made a valuable contribution. Karl Rahner has shown that whenever we are dealing with a mystery, no matter how we express it, we will never say all there is to say about it, never articulate it so as to make it fully plain once and for all. We will continue to reflect on it endlessly, interpreting it in new ways, striving for greater adequacy of understanding and explication.

Within these perspectives we can situate theology today. The theologians we have been reviewing here are trying to do the same service for the faith which others have done before them. They would like to leave people free to take or leave their attempts to express the faith, embracing them if they help, letting them go if they do not.

The contemporary reformulation of Christology will not appeal to everyone. Those who do not find anything of substance in the objections summarized earlier against the Chalcedonian pattern will feel no need to change the classical formulation. And this is fine. The traditional formulation has served the Church well, and will continue to serve many believers well. But those who hear in the objections against the Chalcedonian pattern something of their own difficulties with the tradition, or who hear in the reformulation a clearer statement of what they already believe without having articulated it, will welcome the work that has been done. For them it will be a confirmation of faith, and an encouragement to relate more wholeheartedly to the Jesus in whom they believe.

Those who find contemporary Christology attractive, but wonder if it is authentic New Testament faith and substantially consonant with the tradition of the Church, typically ask questions like the following.

1. How can anyone change the formula of an ecumenical council?

An ecumenical council is itself an exercise in theology, i.e., reflection on faith. The task of theology in every age is, as we have seen, to express the faith in the language of the time.

This is what an ecumenical council attempts to do. This is what the New Testament writers themselves did, interpreting Jesus in the religious categories available to them (most of them coming from the Hebrew Scriptures). Their formulations are normative for all time, since they were the original eyewitnesses and we rely on their testimonies for our access to Jesus. There is no way we can get behind them for a closer look at Jesus, an independent look. So they give us the first and indispensable witness. But this does not mean that we can use no other language than the language they used. Once we have grasped their meaning, we can put it in our own words. The advantage of doing this is that often the message becomes clearer and more compelling.

At an ecumenical council bishops and theologians of a certain age and culture try to express the Christian faith or an aspect of it for their own time. Through discussion and debate, a formulation is finally reached to which at least a majority of those present can say, "That expresses it quite well." And so the formula is adopted. Of course an ecumenical council articulates more than just one person's theological opinion. It is an assembly of representatives from around the Christian world, so that, in a sense, the whole Church speaks in the formula it finally adopts. This is why we take these formulations so seriously, according them normative status.

But every ecumenical council is culturally situated. Its viewpoint is limited, though the Spirit is present to it and works within it. The American Roman Catholic theologian Avery Dulles, who has been a kind of bridge figure between traditional and contemporary formulations, explicates this whole matter of dogma and cultural situation particularly well. He explains that every ecumenical council speaks within the horizons of its time, with the human understanding of the world which its age possesses. It speaks the language that makes sense to the people of that time and culture. It does not answer every question which can be asked about its subject matter, but only the questions which are actually being asked, and often those questions are shaped by very particular debates and controversies, and carry assumptions which go unexamined. A later age may not be asking those questions at all, but different ones. A later age also has a different horizon of understanding, sees the world differently, employs different concepts and language to express what it understands. A later age has different needs. For all these reasons, it has to do theology's task all over again, reflecting on faith, and trying to express it in a manner that is clear and compelling for its time. The Council of Chalcedon was held in the fifth century. Little wonder that we would feel some need for reformulation in the twentieth. In fact, if we simply repeat the words of our forebears in the faith, there is great danger that we will misunderstand them (since the meanings of words change) or not understand them at all (since their whole way of seeing and talking about reality was different). An ossified faith soon becomes an obsolete faith.

In short, it is the evolution of the human race over time that makes it possible to change the formula of an ecumenical council. It makes it not only possible, but necessary if faith is going to continue to make sense and to speak compellingly to each succeeding age.

2. What does the Church teach about Christology today?

The Church has not made an official pronouncement about Christology for a very long time. The Second Vatican Council said nothing about it. The First Vatican Council, which is the next most recent council (1870), said nothing about it. It is hard to say when the next official pronouncement might be. Theologians work all the time. Councils catch up with their work, and endorse it in the name of the whole

Church if it meets conciliar approval. The Second Vatican Council is a good example of this. What it said officially about such matters as liturgy, ecumenism, and the Church in the modern world were all ideas that theologians had been developing for some time. When these ideas and practices first appeared, they seemed innovative, even dangerous or erroneous. But they survived the test of time and were eventually incorporated into the official teaching and practice of the Church.

Many major theologians in the Church today are thinking in the Christological terms we have been considering here. None of their views have been either officially approved or disapproved. If contemporary Christological thinking lacks substance, it will gradually disappear. If it has substance, it will eventually be endorsed. If we wait for a conciliar endorsement of it, we may be waiting for quite some time. We may want to make some decision about where we stand with respect to it beforehand.

3. **In the perspective of contemporary theology, is there any reason why the phenomenon of Jesus cannot occur again in another time and place?**

No contemporary theologian I am aware of speaks of Jesus as a recurrent sort of phenomenon, an instance of something that happens from time to time in human history. No one of them credits other historical individuals as being Jesus' equal, or looks for another in the future. On the contrary, they agree in calling Jesus unique, definitive, unsurpassable. But when it comes to stating why the Jesus phenomenon is unrepeatable, they struggle to come up with a convincing answer. And indeed it does seem to be in principle possible. Yet what is claimed for Jesus by his contemporaries—his perfect union in love and work with God, his divine authority, and his sinlessness—does not seem to have been claimed for any other historical figure.

There are two variables at work in the relationship between God and any historical person, where that person's capacity to be God's self-expression is concerned. One is the extent to which God wishes to communicate self to the person. The other is the extent to which the person wishes to receive and correspond with the divine communication. Our own experience gives us some grasp of the latter variable. We know that we sometimes say yes to God, sometimes no. We know that to some extent we follow the call we feel in ourselves, and that to some extent we ignore it or go against it. We could hardly say of ourselves what Paul says of Jesus:

> Jesus Christ, whom Silvanus, Timothy, and I preached to you as Son of God, was not alternately "yes" and "no"; he was never anything but "yes" (2 Cor 1:19).

We cannot say this of ourselves, but we can at least imagine it. And we know that we do not see it or hear of it in many others. In fact, those we call "saints" were quite convinced they were sinners, i.e., that in many respects they did not correspond with God's initiatives in their lives.

The other variable, God's self-communication, is much harder to track. For when we look at the various degrees of perfection or God-likeness we find in others, we do not know whether the difference is based on God's gift or the person's making capital of the gift whatever its size. Nevertheless, we have some sense of the variations in endowment. We talk about Mary's extraordinary privileges, regarding them as gifts rather than achievements. We talk of the saints' uncommon gifts of prayer, their ecstasies and visions. Some people of our own acquaintance seem to possess certain virtues in a very high degree, and they tell us that they have not worked particularly for them, whereas other people strive mightily and do not do as well. There does seem to be a real difference in the size of the endowment. This would correspond to our experience of other human gifts—physical beauty, health, intellect, emotional stability, etc., which vary greatly from individual to individual. The democratic principle in us objects to this. But here as elsewhere, God's ways do not seem to be ours.

We can understand Jesus, then, in terms of an extraordinary gift of God in the way of self-communication, and an extraordinary correspondence with the gift in the living out of his life, his "obedience," as the New Testament calls it. Why this could not happen again it is very difficult to say. It seems to *have* happened only once.

4. **If what we read in the preceding chapter is the true story of Jesus' life, why don't we find it in the Gospels?**
This is a fair question. It does seem surprising that the true story would not be in the Gospels, but would be waiting for an amateur storyteller in the twentieth century to tell it. But is the story told in the preceding chapter really that different from the story of the Gospels? No, it is partly the same, partly different. Its legitimacy as an extrapolation from the Gospels is rooted in the nature of the Gospels. For the Gospels are not what they at first appear to be, what until recent scholarship we thought them to be, what fundamentalism still erroneously takes them to be. The Gospels are very sophisticated religious documents. Let us take a moment to elaborate this point.

Contemporary biblical scholarship distinguishes three layers of material in the Gospels. This information is now available in many books on the New Testament, but Joseph Fitzmyer in his *A Christological Catechism* does an especially fine job of putting the matter clearly in a few pages. The Gospels represent three stages through which the remembered words and deeds of Jesus passed between their occurrence and the writing of the Gospels. For there was a considerable interval between the life of Jesus and the writing of the Gospels. The earliest Gospel, Mark, was written about 65 A.D. Matthew and Luke were written about 80–85 A.D., and John about 90 A.D. So we are looking at a period of about thirty-five years or more between Jesus' life and the Gospel accounts of it. During this time the memories of him were transmitted orally. What then are the three layers of material in the Gospels?

(1) what Jesus said and did during his earthly life—*the facts*;

(2) the same, but as presented in the disciples' preaching about him after his death and resurrection—*the preaching*;

(3) the same, but as written up by one of the four evangelists in a piece of literature called a Gospel—*the Gospel*.

At each stage of development, the material is modified somewhat. It is modified as it is preached because of the whole new light in which the resurrection has put everything Jesus said and did during his ministry. Now his divinity is clearly seen, and in the light of it his public ministry takes on new significance. Some of his earlier words are understood for the first time. The deeper sign value of his actions shines out from their physical appearance, e.g., the feeding of the multitudes, the healing of blindness, the raising of the dead. Earlier clues to his altogether special relationship with God now stand out lucidly, and his divinity is heightened in the preaching as these stories are recounted, e.g., his baptism, his transfiguration. The situation of the audience, their peculiar questions and needs, also influence the way the material is adapted and presented. The same is true in preaching and teaching today when they are done effectively.

The material is modified again by the evangelist who puts it together in a continuous narrative. He has to make a selec-

tion of stories, because he cannot tell them all. He has to de-
cide what order to put events in, because the exact chronology
of teachings and incidents has been lost by this time. He writes
for a particular Christian community with its peculiar problems and concerns, and this influences both his selection and
the way he edits the material. He has a theological perspective, his own way of understanding the permanent significance
of Jesus, and it colors his whole approach. Of course he is still
working from the bedrock of the words and deeds of Jesus as
handed down. And he is much affected by the interpretation
that has already been given them in the preaching, as well as
the verbal forms that have become fairly standardized. So he
is largely dependent, partly original.

By the time the Gospels are written, the main concern is
the ongoing life of faith. What people are interested in is: Who
is Jesus for us now, and how do we relate to him now? Well,
the Jesus we relate to now is the risen Christ, glorified and
with the Father. Since this is the case, the disciples in their
preaching and the evangelists in their writing feel free to present the words and deeds of the earthly Jesus in their permanent significance for the life of Christians. Thus each Gospel
frame becomes a *typical* frame, one into which I, the believer,
can insert myself in the place of the leper, Zacchaeus, the
woman taken in adultery, the rich young man. And the Jesus
I encounter in that frame is not Jesus precisely as he was in the
original incident in his public life, but Jesus as he is now with
his divinity clearly revealed by the resurrection, since it is
with this Jesus that I the believer now interact. The Gospels
are written in such a way as to meet believers' ongoing needs
for teaching, preaching, and contemplation. They are written
with these ends in view rather than with the object of chroni-
cling with the objectivity of a videotape the words and deeds
of Jesus of Nazareth. They are written by believers for believers, to share a vision of faith. That faith is based in the earthly

history of Jesus, but profoundly influenced by the experience of that same individual risen from the dead and experienced now in glory.

This is why theologians can say today that Jesus did not know the future, and did not fully realize who he was, even though the Gospels present him as predicting his fate in considerable detail and making such statements as: "Before Abraham was, I am" (Jn 8:58), "I am the resurrection and the life" (Jn 11:25), and "The Father and I are one" (Jn 10:30). The Gospels are written from the perspective of resurrection faith, and they put into the mouth of the earthly Jesus words he can utter in truth only as the risen Lord.

Coming back to the story of Jesus as told in the preceding chapter, we can now see that it is not told that way in the Gospels because it is not the Gospels' main interest to chronicle the storyline, record the exact words, or delineate the developing self-consciousness of Jesus. The Gospel writers consider it more valuable for us to present the Christ of faith as we deal with him now, to do it on the matrix of historical recollections but with an overlay of resurrection insight. But we can reconstruct the original story to some extent and guess at the internal experience of the central character with some hope of validity, reading the Gospels with that understanding of them given us by modern biblical scholarship. This is what the preceding chapter attempted to do.

The contemporary understanding of the nature of the New Testament, reached by a very large community of scholars of many Christian denominations over several generations of work, puts us in a position to recognize the error of fundamentalism. Its intentions good, fundamentalism takes the Bible very seriously and so interprets it literally. Biblical scholarship takes the Bible even more seriously, painstakingly uncovering the process by which it came to be and the meanings of its terms as they were understood at the time they were written, so that it can grasp as accurately as possible what God and the human writer were trying to communicate. Because of what it learns in this process biblical scholarship knows better than to interpret the Bible literally as God's very words to us today. It nuances its interpretations of both the Hebrew Scriptures and the New Testament much more carefully, because it knows how very ancient and complex a book the Bible is. When the Bible is read simplistically, it becomes a dangerous book and can do great harm. Fundamentalism reads it simplistically.

5. **How does the contemporary reformulation of Christology affect my relationship to Jesus?**

The reformulation might considerably affect one's image of Jesus. There is a significant shift from "Jesus, God and man" to "Jesus, God in man." It can perhaps be most briefly summarized by saying that one is dealing now with a genuinely human Jesus. The questions for the life of faith then are: Can I still pray to Jesus? Can I worship Jesus? Can I think of Jesus as knowing me personally? Is Jesus still with me? These are important questions.

The answer to all of them is yes. Because God is fully present in Jesus, incarnate in him, when we deal with Jesus we deal with God. When Jesus speaks, God speaks. When Jesus acts, God acts. When I pray to Jesus, I pray to God. When I worship Jesus, I worship God. When I give my life to Jesus, I give it to God. Jesus risen and glorified is still present to me in the Spirit, and this Jesus knows me personally. Jesus is no less God for me than he was in the classical formulation. He makes the same demand on my total commitment, and I can give it with the same complete trust.

While nothing important has been lost in the contemporary reformulation for the ongoing life of faith, something important has been gained. That difficulty of being unable to identify with Jesus' earthly experience has been overcome. Though I relate to someone who is now with God in glory, I know him as one who went through the same earthly pilgrimage I do as a human person just like me. I can find renewed meaning in the words:

> For we have as high priest not one who cannot sympathize with our weaknesses, but one who has been tested in all respects like ourselves, but without sin (Heb 4:15).

6. In contemporary Christology, is Jesus God?

It is interesting how this question has become something of a test of Christian orthodoxy. Jesus did not go around trying to get people to call him God. He just wanted them to repent and open the way for his Father's reign in the world. The New Testament almost never calls Jesus God. Nor does the New Testament call the Spirit God. When the New Testament uses the term "God," with those very few exceptions (three clear cases) where it applies the word to Jesus, it is referring to the Father of Jesus, Yahweh of the Hebrew Scriptures.

When the great German Protestant Scripture scholar Rudolph Bultmann was asked the question "Is Jesus God?" his answer was: Jesus is God for us. This may seem a dodge or an equivocation, but it is actually a carefully nuanced and accurate answer, very much in accord with the New Testament. Its elaboration is what we saw in answer to the last question: The encounter with Jesus is the encounter with God. Jesus is God with us, Emmanuel. "In him dwells all the fullness of the divinity bodily" (Col 2:9). Thus, so far as my relationship with God is concerned, Jesus functions as God for me with full legitimacy. Yet this is not so bald as the statement "Jesus is God." The Hebrew mind thinks functionally. It is the Greek mind that thinks ontologically. The New Testament is a Hebrew book by and large, though under some Greek influence.

It describes Jesus' function for us, and Bultmann summarizes its witness accurately when he says: Jesus is God for us. The early councils, like Nicaea and Chalcedon, attempted to translate this functional witness into a Greek ontology and came up with the formula of two natures in one person, calling Jesus true God. This goes beyond the New Testament.

When Karl Rahner comments on the statement "Jesus is God," he says that it is a true statement. But he points out that the *is* in the statement is not the same kind of *is* as the *is* in "Joe is a man." In the latter case a simple identification is being expressed; in the former it is not.

When contemporary Christology is understood superficially, people sometimes go out and say, "According to the new Christology, Jesus is no longer God!" Or, "Now they are claiming that Jesus is not divine!" Both statements are based on misunderstanding, and do contemporary Christology a grave injustice. Is Jesus divine? Yes, in contemporary Christology Jesus is *very* divine. Is Jesus God? Yes, in contemporary Christology Jesus is God in the sense explained above.

QUESTIONS FOR DISCUSSION

1. How can anyone change the formula of an ecumenical council?
2. What Christology does *the Church* teach?
3. Might the phenomenon of Jesus be repeated in another individual in another time and place?
4. If the story of Jesus told in the preceding chapter is true, why don't we find it in the Gospels?
5. How is your relationship to Jesus affected by the contemporary reformulation?
6. Is Jesus God?

VII. Pre-Existence and Trinity

There are two other questions that are usually asked in response to the contemporary reformulation of Christology: How does contemporary theology understand Jesus' pre-existence, and how does it understand the Trinity? Both of these matters deserve considerable treatment.

PRE-EXISTENCE

The belief that Jesus had some kind of pre-existence in heaven has its root in several texts of the New Testament. Principal among them are the hymn in Philippians and the prologue in John. There are also texts in Colossians and Ephesians which link Christ with creation. Let us examine each of these. But first, a preliminary consideration.

The fundamental premise of contemporary theology is that everything that is said about Jesus is said from the standpoint of our earthly experience of him. Schoonenberg articulates this principle very clearly. We cannot get behind our experience of Jesus to peer into his origins, into some heavenly realm in which he had a pre-history with God. We might know something about it if Jesus himself told us of a pre-history. But he did not. Biblical exegesis today regards sayings of Jesus like "Before Abraham was, I am" (Jn 8:58) as put into his mouth by the believing Church after his resurrection, not as authentic sayings of the historical Jesus. If our only possible standpoint, then, is our experience of the historical Jesus or the risen Christ, what are we saying when we speak of his pre-existence? We are trying to express the conviction that somehow Jesus is from all eternity. There is an extraordinarily intimate relationship between Jesus and God. Jesus is in a unique way God's Son, and everything we know religiously comes to concentration and climax in him. Surely he did not just suddenly spring up in time. He must be part of an eternal divine plan. But nothing that Jesus said about himself nor anything we can deduce with certainty on our own enables us to speak about a personal pre-existence. It is an extrapolation backward from what we experience in the Jesus we know, a kind of logical demand.

Now let us consider the texts which speak of pre-existence.

1. *The Hymn from Philippians*

Your attitude must be that of Christ Jesus.
Though he was in the form of God,
 he did not deem equality with God
 something to be grasped at.
Rather, he emptied himself
 and took the form of a slave,
 being born in the likeness of men.
And being of human estate,
 he humbled himself,
 obediently accepting even death,
 death on a cross.
Because of this,
 God highly exalted him
 and bestowed on him the name
 above every other name,
So that at Jesus' name
 every knee must bend
 in the heavens, on the earth,
 and under the earth,
 and every tongue proclaim

to the glory of God the Father:
Jesus Christ is Lord! (Phil 2:5–11).

This is the well-known kenosis (self-emptying) passage. It has usually been understood as referring to a decision of the Second Person of the Blessed Trinity to empty himself of divinity and descend to earth in human form. Then after earthly life and death, he is exalted again to the position he held before.

Many exegetes and theologians today see the passage differently. They regard it as describing a decision of the earthly Jesus, within his lifetime, to live a lowly servant life rather than a regal one. The two Dutch Roman Catholic theologians, Schoonenberg and Schillebeeckx, interpret the passage along these lines, after exhaustive exegetical study. Not that this is the only possible interpretation of it, but it does have solid exegetical support. According to this exegesis, Jesus found himself with a choice about the basic direction his life would take. Political power was often offered, indeed urged upon him. People wanted to make him king. Even if he did not want that, he had the personal charisms to be a great public celebrity. Given the gifts of personality, intellect, and spirituality Jesus had, he could easily have lived at the top of human society. Indeed it seems that such a person deserves such a life. These were quite possibly Peter's sentiments when he said to Jesus after the first prediction of the passion, "May you be spared, Master! God forbid that any such thing ever happen to you" (Mt 16:22). But Jesus chose differently.

What the hymn in Philippians is expressing in its own way is what the temptation scene in the Synoptic Gospels also expresses. Jesus could have been a provider of bread, a worker of wonders, or a king. None of these would have been evil, and Jesus had to scrutinize them closely to discern whether they were suitable means to the ends he envisioned for his life. His judgment was that they were temptations, that they would pull him off course, that God had in mind for him a different path. And so he renounced them. He followed instead the path of the defenseless prophet and the suffering servant. He chose not to be served, but to serve and to give his life as a ransom for many. It was in this sense that he emptied himself, taking the form of a slave, becoming obedient even unto death. And this earthly choice of the human Jesus is echoed in other New Testament passages.

> Though he was rich, yet for your sake he became poor, so that by his poverty you might become rich (2 Cor 8:9).

> For the joy set before him he endured the cross, despising the shame, and is seated at the right of the throne of God (Heb 12:2).

How are the particular words and phrases in the Philippians passage interpreted in this sense rather than in the sense of a heavenly pre-existence? First, the expression "in the form of God" is understood as "in the image of God," in the same sense that humankind is created in the image of God in Genesis 1. The Greek word in Philippians is the translation of that Hebrew word of Genesis, and need mean nothing more than that word does. It simply means that Jesus, like every human being, was created in the image of God. Then, as to what Jesus regarded as something not to be "grasped at" (rather than "clung to"—the Greek expression could mean either), it is understood as "living on a divine plane"—being "equal to God" in that sense. Schillebeeckx refers here to the temptation of Adam and Eve, that if they ate the forbidden fruit they could "be as gods" (Gen 3:5), and the similar aspiration of those who built the tower of Babel, wanting to have a city with its tower in the sky and so make a name for themselves (Gen 11:

1–9). Jesus looked at the good life which was offered to him (wealth, acclaim, power), this "living on a divine level" as we think of things, and chose not to aspire to it or accept it when offered. Instead, he emptied himself of such possibilities and chose the lowly life of a servant, even to the final extreme of giving his life for others on the cross. This is why God exalts him. Notice that the passage does not say that God *restores* him to his former place, and still less that Jesus *resumes* his former place, either of which would seem possible on the more traditional understanding of the passage. Rather, God exalts him and gives him a name above every other name: Lord.

2. *The Prologue of John's Gospel*

> In the beginning was the Word,
> and the Word was with God,
> and the Word was God. . . .
> And the Word became flesh
> and dwelt among us (Jn 1:1, 14).

How does theology today understand what is being said here? The key question is: What is this "Word"? Everything hinges on that. When the Fourth Gospel is written, we are still several hundred years in advance of those speculations which led to a doctrine of Trinity, of three persons in one God. The New Testament writers speak of Father, of Son, and of Spirit as elements in their experience of God, but they have not hammered out a conceptualization of their nature or relationships. John speaks of the Word. But does he understand Word to mean Second Person of the Blessed Trinity, equal to the Father? It seems most unlikely. The New Testament writers are Jews by background, and they speak a religious language familiar to them from the Hebrew Scriptures. The Hebrew Scriptures know well both the word of God and the spirit of

God, yet they know nothing of a Trinity in our sense. What was this understanding of word of God which led John to call Jesus the Word made flesh?

The word of God was God speaking. God spoke, and the world came to be. The Torah, God's law, was God's word. "Decalogue" (ten commandments) means "ten words." God inspired the prophets, and what they spoke was the word of God. The Hebrew experience of God was an experience of God speaking, expressing self, offering self for a relationship with human beings. This self-expression of God had been going on for a long time before Jesus. It went back as far as humankind could remember. It seemed that God had always been speaking, from the beginning of the world. And so it seemed that the word had been with God from the beginning, and the word was God, i.e., the word expressed God's own selfhood, and the one who encountered the word encountered God.

What did it mean to say that all that had been made had been made through the word? It meant that all creation spoke God.

> The heavens declare the glory of God,
> and the firmament proclaims God's handiwork (Ps 19).

> Since the creation of the world, invisible realities, God's eternal power and divinity, have become visible, recognized through the things God has made (Rom 1:20).

This corresponds with our own religious experience and serves as the basis of much of our contemplation. God speaks in creation, and the word spoken is God. This is a long way from saying that Jesus Christ was personally present at the creation, helping the Father do it.

What did it mean to say that the Word of God became

flesh? Again, the declaration comes out of people's experience of Jesus, not out of a privileged glimpse into what came before human history. The experience is that everything God has ever said is summed up in Jesus. It is all said there, every word. Not only are the teachings of Moses and the prophets cogently summarized in the teaching of Jesus. Everything God wants to reveal about who God is for us is shown in who Jesus is for us. Jesus is not just someone who has occasional words to say to us on God's behalf. He is in all the dimensions of his life God's self-revelation. Thus the word of God was enfleshed in a human life, and in Jesus we beheld the glory of God. This is the Johannine vision as scholars reconstruct it today.

What about passages in Colossians and Ephesians which associate Jesus with the creation? For example:

> All things have been created through him and for him. And he is before all things and all things hold together in him (Col 1:16–17).

The principle of interpretation is the same. These statements are made on the basis of our experience of Jesus in this world, the earthly Jesus of Nazareth, died and risen. What they assert is that in Jesus we encounter something unique in all creation, climactic, central, determinative. His significance is all-embracing. In terms of him, we understand creation and human history anew, from a fresh perspective. God's whole self-revelation is summarized in him, and God's goal for human history pivots around him. The perspective of Colossians and Ephesians is cosmic, and they try to locate the phenomenon of Jesus and his community (it is ca. 85 A.D.) in the context of world history. The thinking is very similar to that of John's Gospel, where Jesus is linked to the cosmic history of God's word.

Overall then, in what sense can we say that Jesus had

some sort of pre-existence? In two senses, as Schoonenberg succinctly summarizes the matter. First, that Jesus was in the plan of God from all eternity, and in the fullness of time he was born. Second, that the word we meet in him is the same word we have already dimly heard before him in other forms, in the creation itself, in the law, in the prophets, in the lives of holy men and women, perhaps even in the pagan philosophers and the founders of other religions. But this word of God spoken to human beings was never spoken so clearly and compellingly as in Jesus of Nazareth, in whom it was enfleshed. Both of these senses of pre-existence are quite different from saying that Jesus himself had a life before he was born.

THE TRINITY

Karl Rahner once remarked that most Christians are tritheists. This means that they believe in three gods. They are trying, of course, to be orthodox, but when they hear the ancient language in which Trinitarian faith is formulated, and process it through the imagination, they come out with three persons conversing with one another. This is not the orthodox doctrine of the Trinity, even if it is the popular conception of it.

Christian theology is humbler today than it has sometimes been. It is tougher-minded about what it will articulate as true, readier to admit how little it knows. A more careful study of Scripture has sobered it. Historical study has instructed it about the contexts of past dogmatic statements. The dialogue with other religions, as well as with thoughtful people at large, has taught it to be more modest about what it says, since such inquirers are not impressed with ideas that carry little intelligibility or stand on weak foundations.

When in the past we spoke about the life of God in eternity, and described how the Son was generated as the Father thought about himself, and then the two looked upon each other with such love that the Spirit was spirated into being, we were speaking of things we knew very little of. These are speculations motivated by love and an understandable interest, but they remain speculations. We cannot know the life of God in eternity. We know God only in relation to ourselves, and the knowledge we have is quite limited. God remains a transcendent mystery. One of Rahner's great contributions to theology is to have insisted indefatigably on this crucial point.

As far as the Trinity in particular is concerned, we know nothing about it and are not even thinking about it until we have the experience of Jesus and of the Spirit released in the Church after his death and resurrection. This is the starting point of our reflection, and must always be our anchor and limitation. We do not know what the life of God was before this or what it is independently of this. If we say that it must always have been so and must always be so because God does not change, we are introducing a principle we cannot substantiate.

What, then, is the experience of God from which our doctrine of the Trinity takes its rise? According to Rahner, we experience God fully incarnate in Jesus of Nazareth on the stage of our history. And we experience God in the depths of our own personhood, empowering us to believe, to hope, to love. We call the first the Son. We call the second the Spirit. The Father is the mystery in the background, never directly experienced, but revealed through Son and Spirit. It is of the Father that John's Gospel says: "No one has ever seen God. The only-begotten Son, who is in the bosom of the Father, has made God known" (Jn 1:18).

There is only one God, and this God remains always mystery to us, even in revelatory experience. God cares for us, and so we call God "Father." How do we know God's care? Because of God's gracious outreach to us in Son and Spirit. We encounter God incarnate in Jesus. This corresponds to our bodiliness. We can touch, see, hear God incarnate, and call him "God the Son" or "Word of God." And we have another experience, God as Spirit. This corresponds to the spiritual dimension of our existence. We encounter God in the depths of ourselves, empowering us spiritually, grounding our faith, hope, and love, endowing us with charisms (1 Cor 12 and 13), making Father and Son present (Jn 15:23), reminding us of the things Jesus said and clarifying them for us (Jn 16:12–14), uniting us with other believers into one social body (1 Cor 12:12–13), praying in us with unspeakable groanings (Rom 8:26–27). This is an experience of God's own self too, occurring in our personal depths. We call it "God the Holy Spirit." God is one, and what we have described is our complex experience of God. It is the basis of our thinking of God as somehow Trinitarian.

It is important to keep in mind that in the classic formulation of our Trinitarian faith, "three persons in one God," "person" does not mean an independent center of consciousness with its own knowing, willing, and freedom, who engages in dialogue with other persons. That is what the word "person" means to us today. But it is not the meaning of those ancient Greek terms (*hypostasis, prosopon*) which the English word "person" has been used to translate. *Hypostasis* means subsistence, a term hard to pin down. *Prosopon* means mask or public persona. Neither is the equivalent of the English "person" in its present psychological sense of an independent center of consciousness. When the classical doctrine is interpreted using "person" in the modern sense, tritheism is the result. For this reason Karl Rahner suggests avoiding the word "person" altogether in teaching and preaching about the

Trinity, using instead "way of being" to translate the ancient Greek terms. Thus God has three "ways of being."

But is there not a genuine dialogue at least between Jesus and the Father, and does this not imply two centers of consciousness? Yes. This dialogue runs all through the life of Jesus. But it is a dialogue between the man Jesus and his God. When you look at what is said between Jesus and God in the Gospels, it would be very hard to understand it in any other way than as a dialogue between a human center of consciousness and a divine center of consciousness.

To come at the doctrine of the Trinity in a slightly different way, D.M. Baillie asks the question: What is distinctive about the Christian God as opposed to the God of other religions? He observes that one of two answers is usually given. The Christian God is love. Or, the Christian God is Trinitarian. Both are good answers. Baillie goes on to explain that the two answers come down to the same thing. Our doctrine of the Trinity means that God is love, i.e., that God chooses not to remain self-enclosed, but to reach out graciously to humankind in Son and Spirit. On this understanding, the doctrine of the Trinity ceases to be an abstract, philosophical, almost mathematical speculation about something far off in the skies which has little to do with us except as a "dogma," three persons in one God. Now we understand it as an articulation of the way we *experience* the graciousness of the mystery we call God (Father) reaching out to us both in human incarnation and in transcendent spirit. That is what Christians were trying to express.

QUESTIONS FOR DISCUSSION

1. How do theologians today understand Jesus' pre-existence? What exactly pre-exists?

2. What is Jesus' relationship to creation on this understanding?

3. What is your position on the question of Jesus' pre-existence?

4. What are the sources of our knowledge of the Trinity?

5. Is Jesus the Second Person of the Blessed Trinity? What does this mean?

6. What relevance does the Trinity have for your day-to-day Christian existence?

VIII. The Resurrection

The resurrection of Jesus is the cardinal affirmation of Christian faith. It is asserted over and over in the New Testament, not only at the end of each Gospel, but in the Epistles and other documents as well. In the Christian liturgical year, Christmas has always been the greatest feast. Besides the immense boost the celebration gets from the commercial interest in it, it is probably cherished in a special way because of the emotional power of a newborn baby, particularly such a child as this. But Jesus' birth would never have come to be so celebrated had it not been for his resurrection from the dead. The resurrection adds immense significance to everything Jesus taught and did, because it gives him an absolutely distinctive status as teacher, wonder worker, and holy man. It is through the experience of the risen Jesus that the Church comes to the clear recognition of who he is. And it is by reason of the resurrection that Jesus is more than an historical memory; it is the basis of his permanent abiding in the Church.

In this chapter we will examine the competing theories of the resurrection, and then look at the significance of the resurrection for our lives.

THEORIES OF THE RESURRECTION

In contemporary theological discussion, the fact of the resurrection is not in dispute. It is around the question of *how* the resurrection occurred, or of exactly what the disciples experienced, that a variety of opinions emerge. There is room for a variety of opinions because no one witnessed the actual resurrection. People found Jesus' tomb empty, and they experienced the risen Lord. But no one saw him rise from the dead. And the accounts of the appearances contain enough discrepancies and difficulties that there is space for speculation. Opinions fall roughly into three classes.

1. **The Resuscitation Theory.** This theory holds that the body of Jesus, which had been laid in the tomb, came to life again and he walked out and revisited the disciples. He ate and drank with them and spoke with them as he always had. After forty days, he ascended into heaven. The resuscitation theory is the literalist position.

In its support this theory can cite the very graphic descriptions of the risen Lord with the disciples, eating a piece of fish (Lk 24), inviting Thomas to put his hand in his open side (Jn 20), making the same sort of clear verbal utterances he always had. And Luke, both in his Gospel (Lk 24) and in Acts (Acts 1), portrays Jesus being lifted up into heaven.

The resuscitation theory labors under formidable difficulties. In the Gospel accounts of the appearances, Jesus typically appears without warning, and then, at the end of an encounter, disappears again. He comes through locked doors. And almost everyone has difficulty recognizing him—Mary at the tomb (Jn 20), the Emmaus disciples (Lk 24), the Apostles who make the great haul of fish (Jn 21). They not only have difficulty recognizing him; they struggle to *believe*. They are repeatedly chided by the risen Lord for their lack of faith (Lk 24). Why should they have any difficulty recognizing him, or have any need to believe, if he came before them just as solidly in the flesh as before? There are other difficulties too. Where does this body of Jesus go when it is lifted up? Where is it now, and how is it sustained? If Jesus is resuscitated and moves about again under the conditions of earthly life, has he really broken through? Is he truly glorified? Can he be present to us all in every time and place?

2. **The Internal Conviction Theory.** This theory holds that after Jesus' death and burial, the disciples were at first in a state of deep shock and disillusionment. But they gradually emerged from this state into a strong internal conviction that Jesus still lived. He had to. No one so beautiful could simply be annihilated. God would not allow someone so good to come to nothing. It was unthinkable. And he himself had trusted so deeply in God. He had to be alive with God now. In fact, many were convinced that they still experienced him, felt he was with them. They could almost speak with him. Surely he lived. In this theory there were no appearances. There was simply a strong internal conviction of faith which came to be shared by a community. To express the strength of it to others, they created vivid stories of his presence with them, and then of his being lifted up.

This is the minimalist position. In a sophisticated age, it is the easiest to believe. None of us has ever seen anyone risen from the dead, and we are disinclined to put much stock in stories of resurrections. On the positive side, many of us can identify with a strong internal conviction that some dear one who has died must still be living and, indeed, even seems in a mysterious way to be still with us. In its support this theory can also cite the discrepancies in the appearance accounts, discrepancies which suggest that it is not solid fact that is being recounted. Besides, no one saw the risen Jesus except believers.

But this theory too has its problems. It seems too reductionist a reading of the very graphic Gospel accounts of Jesus' appearances. It gives no satisfactory accounting for the fact that the appearances take place during only a brief period and then cease altogether, indicating a demarcation of the vivid experiences that certain privileged witnesses had from the common faith experience of the risen Lord in the Church. Paul, in the earliest written testimony to the resurrection that we possess, names a sequence of appearances to specific individuals and groups, and also recounts the end of them:

> He appeared to Cephas, then to the Twelve. After that he appeared to upward of five hundred at the same time, most of whom remain to the present, though some have fallen asleep. After that he appeared to James, then to all the Apostles. Last of all he appeared also to me, as if to one born prematurely (1 Cor 15:5–8).

This passage does not square well with the strong internal conviction theory. The hardest part of the difficulty is Paul himself. Why should he, who is busy persecuting the Church, suddenly and quite on his own develop a strong internal conviction that Jesus of Nazareth is indeed risen and Lord? There is a final difficulty with this theory. On the strength of a purely internal conviction that Jesus must somehow be still alive, unbuttressed by any special experiences of the fact, would the disciples have been able to launch what became a world movement? Would they have been able to convince their hearers and answer their hard questions, whose last indubitable experience had been that of Jesus dead on the cross? Would they themselves have been willing to die martyrs' deaths maintaining this testimony?

3. **The "Spiritual Body" Theory.** This is a middle position. It takes seriously the accounts of the appearances over a limited period of time, though it does not take all the details literally, e.g., eating a piece of fish before their eyes, being lifted up physically into heaven. It understands Jesus to be in a genuinely transformed state, having broken through the limitations of earthly existence, being truly glorified and most in-

timately united with God. It takes the expression "spiritual body" from Paul (1 Cor 15:35–58), who theologizes about the transformation which will take place in all of us in the resurrection, when this corruptible body puts on incorruption, and this mortal body puts on immortality.

This theory seems to offer the most satisfactory interpretation of all the data. It explains the difficulty of recognizing Jesus and the need for faith, as the experience of the risen Lord seems to be a faith experience which, like all faith experiences, can be subsequently doubted. Yet the theory recognizes the genuine difference between vivid experiences of a reality breaking in suddenly and powerfully on people's awareness and the subsequent low-level common faith experience of the Church that the risen Lord lives among us. The "spiritual body" theory squares well with the disciples' experience that after his resurrection the Lord comes to them from glory rather than from a house down the street, and to glory he returns. This is to say that he is with God now, and comes to us from God. This also best explains what happened to Paul on the road to Damascus—something independent of community belief, independent also of a living acquaintance with the earthly Jesus of Nazareth, yet something most powerfully convincing, an encounter with the living Lord.

In this theory, the ascension is understood as a pictorial presentation of Jesus' transition from earthly life to glory. But the resurrection means exactly the same thing, and for most of the New Testament writers the resurrection suffices. Jesus enters his glory when God raises him from death. So these writers do not speak of an ascension. Only Luke does, both at the end of his Gospel and in the first chapter of Acts. It seems to be a literary device for marking the end of the period of special appearances, and of pointing to Jesus' life now in glory with the Father.

Before we leave this matter of the manner of Jesus' resurrection, we should note a few other points. First, what is most important about the resurrection is the *fact* of it, not the how of it. And the fact has massive New Testament testimony, and the firm assent of theologians. The how questions are secondary, technical, and hard to answer definitively. Second, the New Testament says that God raised Jesus from the dead. It never describes the resurrection as something Jesus did for himself, as if he rose up on his own power. The language is that "God raised him," or that Jesus "was raised." On the basis of this more careful reading of Scripture, theologians no longer maintain that Jesus rose from the dead thus proving that he was God. The New Testament language about the resurrection is one of those areas where Jesus and God are clearly distinguished. Jesus is dead and buried. God raises him. Third, it is some sort of bodily resurrection that is attested to. It is not a mere survival of Jesus' soul or spirit. The New Testament says that the tomb is empty, and the appearance accounts present Jesus in some sort of bodiliness, so that there is continuity with his earthly existence even while there is marked transformation. Our hope for ourselves too is in some sort of "resurrection of the body," in the language of the early creeds. This means that we believe in the survival and transformation of our *entire personhood* and in the preservation of all that is really valuable to us, not just in the immortality of our souls after they have shucked off as worthless all that pertains to our lives in this world.

THE SIGNIFICANCE OF THE RESURRECTION

The resurrection of Jesus from the dead operates on several levels of significance. Examining them will make it clear why the resurrection is the cardinal affirmation of our faith.

1. **It validates all that Jesus said and did.** This is no small thing. Jesus was a religious revolutionary, whose claims about how God wanted to be served scandalized the religious leaders of his day and divided the general populace. He thoroughly revised the way his contemporaries thought about the Hebrew Scriptures, the authoritative religious book of his culture. Perhaps that controversy does not particularly concern us, but the question of how God wants to be served does. So does the question of where Jesus fits into God's scheme of things, and Jesus claimed a very significant role. And so does everything that Jesus had to say in his characterization of God as faithful, loving, merciful. All of this was called into question by Jesus' tragic ending. If nothing more had been heard from him, we would be left wondering if he was not perhaps a dreamer, deceived in his fundamental convictions. But God raised him from the dead. This is a decisive vindication of all that Jesus lived and taught.

2. **Only in the resurrection does Jesus become fully himself.** This is true not only in the sense that only in the resurrection does Jesus experience the profundity of his union with God and the full significance of his life. It is true also in the sense that only in their experience of the risen Christ do his disciples recognize the profundity of his union with God and the full significance of his life. The Lord who comes to meet them risen is significantly different from the man Jesus who was their friend and companion. He comes to them from glory, with power and authority, with his divinity fully manifest. The experience amazes them, as it had first amazed him. They had known he was great, but they did not think he was *that* great. They had known he was close to God, but they did not think he was *that* close to God. In the light of this experience of his splendor and transparency to God, they catch his full significance and can now recognize all those subtler hints of divinity

present in his earthly life but not then fully grasped. So when they sit down to write the Gospels, they modify the earthly recollections, embellishing them with the truth they now experience in the resurrection. They want to share with us Christ the Lord in the fullness of his stature.

What is implied here is that the life of Jesus was genuinely a process, as our lives are a process, and that he reached his fullness only when he passed from this world to God. Then and only then did he fully realize who he was and what his life had meant and who God was. The New Testament expresses this process of Jesus' life in many passages, and highlights the significance of his passage through death to risen life. One of the places where we can see it most clearly is in the earliest sermon in Acts, a passage cited earlier.

> Jesus the Nazarene, a *man* publicly shown by God to you through powerful works and portents and signs that *God* did *through* him in your midst, just as you yourselves know; this *man*. . . you fastened to a stake by the hand of lawless men and did away with. But *God* raised him by loosing the pangs of death. . . . Therefore because he *was exalted* to the right hand of God and *received* the promised Holy Spirit from the Father, he has poured out this which you see and hear. . . . Therefore let all the house of Israel know for a certainty that God *made* him both Lord and Christ, this Jesus whom you crucified (Acts 2:22–36; italics ours).

The same sort of "ascending Christology" can be found in the sermons in Acts 3, 4, 5, and 10. This is probably the earliest Christology of the New Testament, and it depicts the gradual unfolding of the fullness of Jesus. This is not meant in the sense that God sees a good man and suddenly decides on the basis of the man's merits to exalt him to the status of Lord and Christ. No, the entire development of the life of Jesus is all by God's initiative and Jesus' response to that initiative. But that life comes into full bloom only in the resurrection.

Paul shows a similar awareness of the decisive advance constituted by Jesus' resurrection.

> . . . the gospel concerning his Son, who was descended from David according to the flesh, but *was made* Son of God in power according to the spirit of holiness *by his resurrection from the dead*: Jesus Christ our Lord (Rom 1: 3–4; italics ours).

We find the same idea in Hebrews, where the humanity of Jesus is graphically portrayed.

> *In the days of his flesh* he offered prayers and supplications with loud cries and tears to the one who could save him from death, and he was heard because of his *reverence*. Although he was a Son, he *learned obedience* through the things that he suffered; and *when he had been made perfect* he became the source of eternal salvation for all those who obey him, *designated* by God as high priest according to the order of Melchizedek (Heb 5:7–10; italics ours).

What the passage seems to be saying is that the earthly Jesus had to struggle with God, as we all do, had to learn obedience the hard way, as we all do, had to pass through trials and even the agony of death before he could become fully the source of unending salvation for others. This corresponds with our own experience of having to live awhile and suffer some things and win through them before we can be much help to others. It corresponds with the deliberate subjection of the aspiring shaman of other religions to a taxing series of trials including the "sweat house" before he is recognized as a leader. And it suggests an answer to the so-called "mystery of the hidden life" of

Jesus. Why did Jesus wait thirty years before he came out and started preaching? Because he had to live awhile first. He had to gain some life experience and mature before he could have something worthwhile to say, and before he could get anyone to pay any attention to him.

Our main point here is that the resurrection is Jesus' fulfillment. The transformation and crowning of all that had gone before is of the greatest significance both for him and for his followers. He and they both experience more than just his being alive again whereas he had been dead. He is significantly different, glorified, one with God, as he appears to them invested with divine power and glory.

3. **The resurrection is Jesus' transition into a new mode of existence, existence in the Church through the Spirit.** There is another motif that runs through the post-resurrection New Testament writings. And as the appearances die away, it becomes the dominant motif. Christ lives in the Church. He is with us always, in the community, among us and in each of us, present to us also in word and sacrament. This means that he has a new mode of existing. The resurrection marks a transition from individual historical existence to a new spiritual presence in a community of persons. Where the incarnation had been in the individual, Jesus of Nazareth, the incarnation now is in the social group called Church. God was in Christ. God in Christ is now in the Church, through the Spirit.

> If you love me and obey my commandments, I will ask the Father and he will give you another Paraclete, to be with you always: the Spirit of truth, whom the world cannot accept, since it neither sees him nor recognizes him; but you can recognize him because he remains with you and will be within you. I will not leave you orphans; I will come back to you. A little while now and the world will see me

no more; but you will see me because I live and you will live. On that day you will know that I am in my Father, and you in me, and I in you (Jn 14:15–20).

This passage speaks of the gift of the Spirit, whom, Jesus says in the same discourse, he will send them when death takes him away. In fact, he says, he *must* go to be able to send them the Spirit (Jn 16:7). This designates the transition from one mode of his presence with them to another, from the concrete historical to the spiritual. But, as we can see in the passage quoted above, it is not a straight substitution of Spirit for Jesus. Jesus says that he himself is coming back and will be in them. And then he mentions the Father, too, in whom he lives. So he will continue to be with them himself, but in a new mode, in the Spirit.

This transition, which happens in the death/resurrection of Jesus, is the basis of the Pauline theology of the Church as the body of Christ. And as he speaks of it he speaks both of Christ and of the Spirit.

The body is one and has many members, but all the members, many though they are, are one body; and so it is with Christ. It was in one Spirit that all of us, whether Jew or Greek, slave or free, were baptized into one body. All of us have been given to drink of the one Spirit . . . . You (plural), then, are the body of Christ. Every one of you is a member of it (1 Cor 12:12–27).

This is the chapter in which Paul speaks of the various charisms the Spirit gives to individual members of the body for the life of the totality. Thus it is his basic description of the Church—an organism animated by the Spirit, the ongoing incarnation of Christ in history.

When does the Church come into existence? We have sometimes pinpointed it as that moment during the earthly ministry when Jesus said to Peter: "Thou art Peter, and upon this rock I will build my Church" (Mt 16:18). Exegetes today seriously question whether this really happened during the earthly ministry; they find good reasons for thinking it is a post-resurrection happening retrojected back into the ministry. It is remarkable, for instance, that if this is such an important moment for the future of the Church, only Matthew, of the four evangelists, mentions it, and Paul seems to know nothing about it either. Others would identify the origin of the Church with the day of Pentecost, when the Spirit is poured out. That is the Lukan version. But in John, the Spirit is given by Jesus in one of the post-resurrection appearances.

> At the sight of the Lord the disciples rejoiced. "Peace be with you," he said again. "As the Father has sent me, so I send you." Then he breathed on them and said: "Receive the Holy Spirit" (Jn 20:20–22).

In fact, in John Jesus seems to give the Spirit even as he dies. There is a play on words in the line which describes Jesus' death. What has often been translated "He gave up the ghost" can just as well be translated "He handed over the Spirit."

> When he had taken the vinegar, Jesus said: "It is finished." And bowing his head, he handed over the Spirit (Jn 19:30).

This is consistent with the whole theology of the Fourth Gospel, in which Jesus' passion and glorification are one. His being "lifted up" designates both his crucifixion and his exaltation in glory, the one through the other. So the handing over of his Spirit to the Church fits well for John at this point.

In sum, it is difficult if not impossible to pinpoint the moment of the coming into being of the Church. We would have to say that the Church begins to come into being as Jesus begins gathering his first disciples. It is not completely in being until Jesus has passed through death and been raised again to a new mode of existence, both personal with the Father in glory and incarnate still in the world through the Spirit in the community of those who belong to him.

Paul virtually identifies Christ and the Spirit in their presence in the Church.

> The Lord is the Spirit, and where the Spirit of the Lord is, there is freedom. All of us, gazing on the Lord's glory with unveiled faces, are being transformed from glory to glory into his very image by the Lord who is the Spirit (2 Cor 3:17–18).

This, then, is the third dimension of the significance of the resurrection of Jesus. It is a transition into a new mode of being, so that he is still present in the world spiritually, in that social body of his which we call the Church.

There is a fourth dimension of significance in the resurrection. That is its permanent significance as a paradigm or model of life coming out of death. The resurrection becomes the basis of our hope as we face the many kinds of death we have to die, not only that final frightening death of our bodies, but all those lesser deaths that come to us in the course of our lives through failure, loss, frustration, and other forms of diminishment. The resurrection of Jesus from the dead grounds our courage and our hope in these events. Our hope is in that God whom Paul characterizes as the one "who restores the dead to life and brings into being the things that are not" (Rom 4:17). This important dimension has already been developed in the chapter on salvation.

QUESTIONS FOR DISCUSSION

1. What are the three broad interpretations of the disciples' experience of Jesus risen? What are the strengths and weaknesses of each position? What is your position?
2. What happened to Jesus in the resurrection, as far as we can tell?
3. What importance does the resurrection have for Christian existence?

IX. Jesus in Liberation Theology

One of the most significant theological movements to emerge in the last twenty years is that of liberation theology. It originated in Latin America, and is shaped distinctively by the Latin American situation. Among its leading figures are Gustavo Gutierrez, Juan Luis Segundo, Leonardo Boff, and Jon Sobrino. Gutierrez was the first to describe the context, intent, and principles of the movement in his *Theology of Liberation*. Segundo has applied it to several different areas of theological concern in his five-volume *Theology for Artisans of a New Humanity*. Boff, in *Jesus Christ Liberator*, and Sobrino, in *Christology at the Crossroads*, have each written a liberation Christology. The whole movement merits our attention because in it are heard voices distinctively different from the European and North American voices which have so long shaped our theological thinking.

In this chapter we will focus on liberation Christology, relying principally on Boff and Sobrino. We will describe the context of liberation Christology, then chart its main emphases, then develop its understanding of the kingdom, and finally look at the peculiar way it views the career of Jesus.

THE CONTEXT OF LIBERATION CHRISTOLOGY

Every Christology is done in a situation. It develops in a dialogue between two poles: the New Testament record and

Christian tradition on the one hand, and the cultural context of the person who reflects on them on the other. When Christology is done well, Jesus is presented in such a way that people feel their problems are being discussed (a valuable cue for preaching also). We saw this point earlier in assessing the significance and limitations of an ecumenical council. Every age and every culture read the basic story differently, finding different shades of existential meaning in it according to the different questions and concerns that people bring to the text.

The cultural situation of Latin America shows variations from country to country, but there are some common characteristics. Hunger, unemployment, inhuman living conditions, infant mortality, and endemic diseases are the facts of life for the vast majority of the people. And there is little recourse. Wealth is concentrated in the hands of a few, and these maintain the government. Both government and wealthy are defended by a vast army of police and soldiers whose work is finely tuned by a central intelligence agency. The network of oppression is larger still, international in scope. For there are other nations and multinational corporations who have a strong interest in maintaining conditions exactly as they are. They want both the cheap natural resources and the cheap labor. And they want peace, not turmoil or revolution, because commerce proceeds with difficulty when conditions are unstable, and profits would be greatly affected were justice to prevail. Under these social and economic conditions it is not surprising that political prisoners fill the jails. They are those who have raised a voice against the dehumanization that weighs so oppressively on the populace. What makes the Latin American situation the more poignant is that Latin America is ninety percent or more Christian. The small number who possess all the wealth are Christians. The government officials who maintain the status quo are all Christians. And the professional torturers and death squads who "keep the peace" are all Christians too.

It is in this situation that liberation Christology is born. In the words of Jon Sobrino, it views classical Christology as a "sublime abstraction," because classical Christology has been the faith of all these people for generations and it has never touched the cultural situation. It floats easily above it in an abstract realm. It expresses itself in a popular religiosity of processions, devotions, and sacramental rituals which leave everything unchanged. Was this what Jesus was about? Liberation Christology answers a decisive no. It maintains that what has been forgotten is the historical Jesus, his teachings about wealth and poverty and social relationships, his labors to bring all people freedom and life, and the cruel fate he met as a result of both. Liberation Christology sees a striking similarity between the historical situation of Jesus and the historical situation in which it operates today. Jesus too lived in a situation of bondage, injustice, and oppression, in a highly stratified society in which power was used to oppress rather than to serve. He confronted the powers, espousing the cause of the oppressed. His energies were dedicated to the cause of liberation. In every sense of the word, he can be called "Liberator."

THE EMPHASES OF LIBERATION CHRISTOLOGY

We can get a deeper sense of the spirit of liberation Christology by noting some of its main emphases. They can be made most clear in a series of contrasts.

1. **The Historical Jesus over the Christ of Faith.** The Christ of faith is the divine figure who represents for each individual the compassionate and merciful love of God. This is valid, but it can be overemphasized at the expense of other di-

mensions. It can foster an abstraction from the Jesus of history. The Jesus of history looked around angrily at the scene he found in the temple, and he held a whip in his hand. The Jesus of history told the parable of Lazarus and Dives and of the good Samaritan. The Jesus of history pronounced woe to the rich, and called the poor and meek blessed. The Jesus of history confronted the authorities of his day for imposing heavy burdens on people and not moving a finger to lift them, and religious authority in particular for outward show and hypocritical inconsistency. Liberation Christology insists that we remember the Jesus of history, and not let him disappear in the Christ of religious devotion.

2. **Discipleship over Religion.** Jesus calls us not to be religious, but to follow him. He calls us not to say Lord, Lord, but to love our neighbor. He enlists our energies not for processions and cultic ceremonies, but for the task of rebuilding human society in such a way that the oppressed are freed and the suffering helped, so that all can have life and have it abundantly. Discipleship means following in his footsteps, living his values, joining his labors. Discipleship means living the great commandment, putting our trust in God instead of in wealth and material securities, and loving our neighbor in practical concern and service. Religion can mean many things. Too often it means an escape into a spiritual realm and into peculiarly religious activities. It measures itself by standards of orthodoxy and spiritual devotion.

3. **Orthopraxis over Orthodoxy.** "Ortho" means straight or true, as in "orthodontics." "Praxis" means practice or action, and "doxy" means opinion or belief. Liberation Christology puts the accent on true living rather than true believing. It says simply that what you do is more important than what you say you believe, your orthopraxis is a much more authentic test of your Christianity than your orthodoxy. What is im-

portant is not the doing of Christology but the following of Christ. This is true, of course. What these theologians sometimes forget to say is that the way you do Christology has a lot to do with the way you are a disciple, because orthodoxy determines the particulars of orthopraxis. But the valid point they make is that orthodoxy, important though it is, is not enough for being a Christian. And they add another note. The only way to know Jesus is to follow him. You have to get onto the path of discipleship. You cannot know him by studying doctrine.

4. **Communal over Individual Spirituality.** The Christian has to think community. *We* are the body of Christ. We have to be mindful of our interrelatedness and have at heart the welfare of all. Our love has to be as universal as the love of Christ. To espouse a "Jesus and I" spirituality is to forget so much of the teaching of Jesus and the reality of the body of Christ. The issue is not individual salvation alone but the salvation of the world. When Peter thrice confesses his love for Jesus, Jesus' rejoinder is not, "Then come apart with me," but "Feed my lambs" (Jn 21). Those who love the Lord are always missioned by him to serve others. The characteristic way that the emerging Latin American church is organizing to exercise this kind of social concern is in the form of base communities. These are manageable-size groups of people who form genuine community with each other, meeting regularly to reflect on what the message of the Gospel is for their situation, taking action together, and looking out for one another's welfare. These base communities are the model for what these Christians labor to achieve in the human community at large. What they strive both to model and to realize in all of human society is the reign of God. The reign of God is a key New Testament concept, and the pivotal theological concept of the liberation movement. To it we turn next.

LIBERATION THEOLOGY'S CONSUMING PASSION: THE REIGN OF GOD

The key to understanding the spirit of liberation theology is to grasp the way it views the reign of God. The "reign of God" is synonymous with the "kingdom of God," or even the "kingdom of heaven" (Matthew's version of the phrase), an expression constantly on the lips of Jesus in the Gospels. It is the subject of many of his parables, and the framework within which he sets his ministry, his first words in Mark being: "The appointed time has been fulfilled, and the *reign of God* is at hand. Reform your lives, and believe the good news" (Mk 1:15, italics ours). With many others, we translate the New Testament expression "reign" rather than "kingdom" because "reign" is a more dynamic term, free of the structured, geographical connotations of "kingdom." Thus it is closer to the sense of the original metaphor in Jesus' preaching, a metaphor for which his favorite substitution seems to be a seed that grows.

Liberation theology rehabilitates the New Testament idea of the reign of God, pointing out how central it is in the preaching of Jesus. Jesus preached neither himself nor the Church, but the reign of God, which was his consuming passion. He said that the reign of God was at hand. What is this reign of God?

According to liberation theology, the reign of God is a whole new social order. Christians have sometimes lived as if the reign of God was heaven, life after death. Liberation theology insists, on the basis of solid exegesis, that the reign of God has both a this-worldly and a next-worldly dimension. It is a seed planted in this world, intended to grow in this world and to come to fulfillment in the hereafter. Jesus inaugurates the reign of God with the religious and social revolution he brings both in his preaching and in his activity. With a clarion call to repentance and conversion, he works to overcome all the alienations and injustices in human society, radically changing the way human beings relate to God and to each other. Paul sums up Jesus' work this way:

> There is neither Jew nor Greek, there is neither slave nor free person, there is neither male nor female; for you are all one in Christ Jesus (Gal 3:28).

> If anyone is in Christ, they are a new creation. The old order has passed away; now all is new (2 Cor 5:17).

The reign of God is not a territory but a new order. It involves reconciliation, healing, and the overcoming of everything that is inimical to God and humankind, in other words, sin and all the social effects of sin. Jesus tells his disciples to stop asking when or where it is going to appear, for it is already in their midst (Lk 11:20). The signs of it are that the blind see and the lame walk and the poor have good news preached to them, i.e., oppression and suffering are being overcome and people are being freed to live fuller and more joyful lives.

Jesus issues a call to repentance and conversion because the reign of God demands a complete revolution in the way one sees the world and behaves. He tells people to sell all they have and give to the poor. He replaces the stipulations of law with love as the standard of human conduct. It is a less controlled approach and at the same time a more demanding one, because love's work is never done whereas one can say one has done everything the law commands. Jesus sets aside the law whenever what people really need constitutes a higher value than the value enshrined in the law. He is himself free, and he sets others free. The reigning authorities, not just political but religious, do not like either what he teaches or what he does. But what he teaches and lives is the reign of God, which calls the entire existing order into question.

Liberation theology not only rehabilitates the notion of the reign of God; it gives the notion this fresh interpretation. It will not allow it to be etherealized into the heaven that awaits us after we die, or even into a purely spiritual reality while we live in this world. Neither of these really touches the temporal order, and liberation theology rightly insists that the reign of God in Jesus' preaching and action had decisive impact on the temporal order. For Jesus, the reign of God was the seed that grows secretly in this world, the leaven in the dough, the banquet that begins now and continues in the hereafter. The reign of God was the teaching and activity he himself began and missioned others to continue, going to the ends of the earth to heal, to reconcile, to form communities. The reign of God begins here and now. "See, I make all things new. . . . It is already done" (Rev 21:5–6).

LIBERATION THEOLOGY
AND THE CAREER OF JESUS

Liberation Christology is much more interested in what Jesus taught and labored to accomplish and in the fate he met as a result than it is in precise questions about Jesus' divinity. To the extent that it does address these latter questions, it takes various positions. Boff sees Jesus as the incarnation of God in the classical sense, though he emphasizes the humanity of Jesus more than classical Christology usually has. Sobrino takes a somewhat different position, seeing Jesus not as the revelation of the Father but as the revelation of the Son. Sobrino perhaps goes a little too far in stressing this point, losing thereby the important ways Jesus makes the Father known to us. But what he emphasizes is a valid point. Jesus reveals to us what it means to correspond with God (the Father). He is the way; he is the servant of God; he is the Son. He points toward and leads toward the Father, our future, the one whose reign is yet to be revealed in its fullness. The call of Jesus in Sobrino's Christology is not a call toward himself as goal but toward himself as leader. Jesus wants us to fall in behind him in laboring to realize the reign of God in our own lives and in the world and in this way to move by faith toward God. Sobrino's fear is that as soon as we make Jesus God, we rest in worship and lose our way. The history of Christianity in so much of Latin America is the basis of this fear. This is why Sobrino stresses that Jesus preached not himself and not the Church but the reign of God.

Liberation Christology portrays Jesus as a man of faith and of prayer, one who sought the will of God in his life and strove to accomplish it even when failure pressed in on every side and God's purpose was hidden from him. Citing Hebrews 12:2, which calls Jesus the "pioneer and finisher of faith," these theologians see Jesus as the model par excellence of faith. In trial and temptation, he maintained his trust and obedience.

Liberation Christology frames the condemnation and death of Jesus as flowing inevitably from the way he lived. This view stands in contrast with others which see Jesus as having come down from heaven to die and thus to accomplish the redemption of the human race. In liberation thought, Jesus' life and the kind of death he died are in continuity, the latter flowing almost necessarily from the former. Jesus was a prophet, and prophets are almost always murdered. He was a witness to the truth, and the truth threatened the interests of many, and they wanted to get rid of him. He was very popular with the masses, and his popularity provoked jealousy and hatred among those who felt themselves eclipsed. The way he broke the law, criticized existing authority, and spoke intimately of God was all very threatening, and it stirred up the populace. He was a troublemaker. So they arrested him, interrogated him, tortured him, condemned him in a mock trial, and gave him the death penalty. The pattern is a very familiar one, particularly in Latin America today. It is a creation of human wickedness, not of God's design at all.

The way Jesus pursues his course in the face of danger, and the way he submits to his unjust and cruel fate, all to further the reign of God, becomes the inspiration of the liberation movement. At earlier stages in his life Jesus had taken steps to avoid death, though never either by use of force or by backing down on what he was doing. At this point, he has to submit to it. In the face of the evil powers now marshaled against him and his lifework, he chooses not to take up the sword, nor to gather an army, though many urge him to do so. He "entrusts himself to the one who judges justly" (1 Pet 2:23), asking forgiveness from the cross for those involved in this deed. To the end, he endeavors to overcome evil with love. He makes a sacrifice of his life.

But as Christians struggle for the liberation of Latin America, and meet such cruel reprisals, they cannot help asking the pained question: Where is God in all this? How can God stand by and watch this? It leads them to a deeper contemplation of the crucifixion of Jesus. If Jesus is God's Son and faithful Servant, how can God stand by as all his dreadful tragedy unfolds? Liberation's answer is that God suffers as love with Jesus in this situation, and cannot do anything else, given the way God has chosen to exercise power in the world. God respects human freedom and never violates it. God leads the world with the divine vision of goodness and truth, but never imposes any other kind of force. Here liberation theology shows a similarity to process thought, as well as to some of Bonhoeffer's thinking. It sees Jesus dying on the cross as the revelation of God, for God is suffering love, using persuasive power, never coercive power, in the world. Jesus lives the weakness of God and is crucified with God in the world, using no other power than that of love and truth. God suffers as love, working *within* the negativities of sinful human history. God immerses self in our pain, and triumphs from within it. So it is not a question of what God could be doing and for some reason is not. This is who God is and what kind of power alone God uses. This seems to be what Paul is getting at in his discussion of power and weakness, wisdom and foolishness, in 1 Corinthians.

> The message of the cross is complete absurdity to those who are headed for ruin, but to us who are experiencing salvation it is the power of God. . . . Yes, Jews demand "signs" and Greeks look for "wisdom," but we preach Christ crucified, a stumbling block to Jews and an absurdity to Gentiles; but to those who are called, Jews and Greeks alike, Christ the power of God and the wisdom of God. For God's foolishness is wiser than men, and God's weakness is more powerful than men (1 Cor 1: 18–25).

Liberation Christology expects that those who follow Jesus will meet his fate. His way is the way of the cross; it is the only way that sin and sin's effects in the world can be overcome. It is God's way. But the resurrection of Jesus is the basis of liberation's hope and courage in the face of the suffering it undergoes. The reign of God does grow even in apparent failure and defeat. God transforms our work. Justice and love increase. And the victim somehow wins out over his murderer.

These are the main accents and emphases of liberation Christology. We treat it because it is fresh and because it is distinctive. It should be evident how greatly liberation theology enriches our Christological reflection, especially in the area of Jesus' teaching on wealth and poverty, on power, and on the reign of God. This school of theology demonstrates quite convincingly that "politics" *do* have a place in "religion," at least in Christian religion. And it shows the intimate connection between working for justice in an unjust world and suffering persecution and death. As we study liberation Christology, we may get the uncomfortable impression that the finger is being pointed at us, and indeed it may. It is easy to be part of oppressive structures if we benefit from them. The call to conversion so eloquently expressed in this theology is a call that God may be addressing to us.

QUESTIONS FOR DISCUSSION

1. What is liberation theology? How is it shaped by its cultural context?
2. What are the main accents in liberation theology's treatment of Jesus' life, teaching, death, and resurrection?
3. What is your evaluation of liberation Christology? What implications, if any, does it have for your life?

X. Christianity Among the Religions of the World

As Christian believers who love Jesus, we find ourselves naturally interested in all the issues we have considered so far—the salvation Jesus brings, the meaning of discipleship, Jesus' relationship with God, his life and teaching, his death and resurrection. Before we close this study of him, it might be good to look up from our work and ask ourselves a different question, one that arises from the situation of religious pluralism within which we live. What is our relationship to people who do not share our faith? What is the relationship between Christianity and the other religions? Let us focus the question quite precisely. How important is Jesus for the salvation of the world?

There are two basic positions on how central Jesus Christ is in bringing human beings salvation. One is that all salvation comes from him and him alone. The other is that he is just one among many mediators of salvation. Each of these two basic positions has some shadings, and we will examine each of them in the course of our development.

What is salvation? It is many things, as we saw in the first chapter. The most crucial sense of it for the present discussion is life after death. The question is whether a person can get to heaven or not without faith in Jesus Christ. The secondary concern would be whether a person could enjoy the benefits of some kind of salvation in this world without Jesus Christ, i.e., some kind of contact with God, some experience of God's graciousness (the meaning of the term "grace"), some help with the problems of the human situation.

Let us consider each of the basic positions on the tie between salvation and Jesus Christ.

JESUS CHRIST IS THE EXCLUSIVE MEDIATOR OF GOD'S SALVATION

This position has a long tradition and can claim a number of New Testament texts in its support.

> And he said to them: "Go into all the world and preach the good news to all creation. The man who believes and is baptized will be saved; the man who does not believe will be condemned" (Mk 16:15–16).

> Furthermore, there is no salvation in anyone else, for there is not another name under heaven that has been given to men by which we must be saved" (Acts 4:12, sermon by Peter).

> Jesus said: "I am the way, and the truth, and the life. No one comes to the Father except through me" (Jn 14:6).

> For there is one God, and one mediator between God and men, the man Jesus Christ (1 Tim 2:5).

The conviction that Christianity is the one true religion, and sometimes even more exclusively that the Roman Catholic Church is the one true Church, has led to great missionary efforts throughout the world in all the Christian centuries. The conviction has led, less happily, to religious wars, to persecutions, and to the use of force to bring conversions. The theology underlying all these activities has various shadings.

The most exclusive reading of it is that one must be explicitly a member of the Church, and so one must be baptized. This too has New Testament underpinnings. In addition to the Marcan text cited above, there is the Johannine text:

> Jesus answered: "Most truly I say to you, unless a man is born from water and the spirit, he cannot enter the kingdom of God" (Jn 3:5).

To name but one Christian missionary who worked out of this theology, St. Francis Xavier in the sixteenth century spent his life among the people of the Orient, giving basic Christian instruction and baptizing. A man of tremendous zeal and energy, he moved through India and Japan, and died off the coast of mainland China, in sight of his next great project. He was driven by a consuming love for Christ and by Christ's own love for human beings. But by his own admission, he worked out of the conviction that by baptism he was snatching as many souls as he could from hell. He stands within this first theological position.

A less exclusive position holds that persons might be saved outside the Christian Church, but that the salvation which reaches them is mediated through the Church, because all salvation comes through Christ and he extends it to people through the Church. This theology may or may not speculate on how that salvation reaches people who are not members of the Church. One theory is that the Church has at least to some extent Christianized human culture.

A still less exclusive position holds that salvation is ultimately from Christ, but that it reaches some people quite without the mediation of the Church. Thus it is not necessary either to be a member of the Church or even to be culturally under the influence of the Church. Christ can reach people with his grace independently of the Church he founded. This theology does not usually explain how. It relies implicitly on an identification of Christ with God. As God is omnipresent, so is Christ. Where God is active, Christ is active.

What all three of these variant positions have in common is that all salvation comes through Christ. They differ in the degree of involvement of the Church as the mediator of Christ's salvation.

Some theologians today are abandoning this exclusivist position and moving to the more open stance that Jesus Christ is only one mediator of salvation among others. There are essentially three considerations that persuade them to do this.

The first is the realization that there are many good people who lie outside the Christian pale. When Christians live in Christian ghettos, they do not have significant contact with these people. But when under conditions of modern mobility the ghettos dissolve and people of all kinds are mixed together, a puzzling experience breaks in quite powerfully. One works next to a professed atheist who is a person of high moral quality. One goes to school with a Jew, Hindu, or Muslim who is not only morally upright but religiously devout. These people seem to have a very lively relationship with God. How can this be? They do not draw their inspiration from Jesus Christ; they may know very little of him, and feel no need to learn more. Yet they live very impressive lives. It becomes embarrassing as well as puzzling when these people are clearly living better lives than many Christians.

The second experience comes to those who do studies in comparative religion. They read the inspired writings of other religions and dialogue with their members. The sacred writings seem genuinely inspired and uplifting. The ethics stressed in the writings and teachings of the non-Christian religions are essentially the same as the ethics found in the writings and teachings of Christianity, and they are lived in similar ways. Dogmas differ, and rituals differ, but the ways of life observable across the religious spectrum do not show significant differences. William Johnston, a Christian theologian who has lived for years among Japanese Zen Buddhists and written extensively of the dialogue between Zen Buddhism and Christianity, notices that when Christians and Zen Buddhists silently meditate together, they all seem to be in contact with the same mysterious reality, and they do very well discussing their religious experiences together. It is when they begin discussing dogma that they cannot agree. Mysticism unites the various religions. Common action to meet human needs also unites them. Dogma divides. This raises some questions. How important is dogma? And how valid is it? When we move from our religious experiences, which are always encounters with mystery, to articulating them in creed, code, and cult, the staples of organized religion, we move from surer to shakier ground. At any rate, the study of comparative religion and actual contact with the adherents of non-Christian religions cast doubt on the premise that Jesus Christ is the only source of salvation.

The third consideration is the conundrum of the world religious picture in the late twentieth century. Putting it very roughly, the world is about one-third Christian at the present time. Approximately half of this third, or one-sixth of the world, is Roman Catholic. The other two-thirds is non-Christian, five-sixths non-Catholic. This is after two thousand years of missionary effort. If you take the exclusivist position that salvation is attainable only through faith in Jesus Christ, then two-thirds of humanity is damned, five-sixths if your requirement is that one be a Roman Catholic. This raises a very acute question about God. What kind of God is it who creates the vast majority of human beings for eternal damnation? Don't

Christians preach a God of immense love? Are these people to be blamed for the fact that they are not Christians?

These are the considerations that lead to the more open Christian position on salvation, to which we now turn.

JESUS CHRIST IS ONE MEDIATOR OF SALVATION AMONG OTHERS

What many Christians do not realize is that this position too can appeal to texts of the New Testament.

> At this Peter opened his mouth and said: "For a certainty I perceive that God shows no partiality, but in every nation the man that fears God and does what is right is acceptable to God" (Acts 10:34–35).

> As I walked about looking at your shrines, I even discovered an altar inscribed "To a God Unknown." What you are worshiping without knowing it, that I proclaim to you" (Acts 17:23, Paul's sermon in Athens).

> For it is not those who hear the law who are just in the sight of God; it is those who keep it who will be declared just. When Gentiles who do not have the law keep it as by instinct, these people although without the law serve as a law for themselves. They show that the demands of the law are written in their hearts. Their conscience bears witness together with the law, and their thoughts will accuse or defend them on the day when, in accordance with the gospel I preach, God will pass judgment on the secrets of men through Christ Jesus (Rom 2:13–16).

> God wants all men to be saved and come to the knowledge of the truth (1 Tim 2:3–4).

This explains why we work and struggle as we do; our hopes are fixed on the living God who is the savior of all men, but especially of those who believe (1 Tim 4:10).

God is love, and he who abides in love abides in God and God in him (1 Jn 4:16).

These texts loosen the hold of the exclusivist position and of the fear or fanaticism that sometimes attends that position. They depict a God whose salvific intent is universal, and the signs of whose saving action are perceivable in persons outside the Christian community, perhaps outside the entire field of force of Jesus Christ.

One could hold this sort of latitude about salvation and still maintain that where there is salvation it is due to the influence of Jesus Christ, even if Christ is not acknowledged. But theologians of a more empirical cast of mind find this position unconvincing. They see no positive evidence that it comes from Jesus Christ. They take seriously the testimony of the people concerned, who say they never heard of Jesus Christ or at least do not know his life or teaching well. They draw their religious inspiration from other sources. Thus it seems that Jesus Christ is one mediator of God's salvation among others.

There are two variations of this basic position. The first holds that although Jesus Christ is not the exclusive mediator of salvation, he is the normative mediator. This means that he is the highest, the fullest, the most complete, and hence the norm by which all other mediations are to be measured. This is the position Paul Tillich takes. There is in Jesus a unique fullness of God and God's salvation. All other forms of salvation are only approximations, falling in some measure short and needing to be filled out or corrected by his. This position usually bases itself on the strong claims that the New Testament makes for Jesus and his relationship with God. Sometimes it also attempts to show from a comparative study of all the religions that the Christian religion is particularly rich, balanced, and inclusive of all that is true and good in the other religions.

The other variation of the one-among-many position holds that Jesus Christ is indeed a mediator of salvation but that it cannot be shown that he is superior to the others and therefore normative. He may be, but no human being can get into a sufficiently objective position to evaluate the religious founders and their religious systems and declare which is the greatest. The New Testament comes from a particular point of view. It is culturally situated and culturally limited. It cannot rise to a universal viewpoint. The contemporaries of Jesus did not know the whole world and its many religions, nor all the holy men and women of all cultures so that they could situate Jesus among them. Their statements are necessarily relative, as all human statements are relative, even those in which divine inspiration is a component. As far as the statements of comparative religionists are concerned, those people who have found Christ and Christianity to be the greatest have all been Christians. Their objectivity is called into question by their initial bias. To try another objective standard, if Christianity were clearly the richest and most balanced religion, wouldn't the other religions in two thousand years' time come to recognize this fact and converge on it as the center? This has not happened, nor does it seem to be happening.

THEOLOGICAL UNDERPINNINGS
OF THE MORE OPEN POSITION

Besides the Scripture texts which can be adduced in favor of the second basic option, there is a more encompassing theological understanding which serves as its context. The insight is that the reality of God is not exhausted in the reality of Jesus Christ, i.e., that God and Jesus cannot be simply identified. The reality of God is larger than the reality of Jesus. God's Word was being heard before Jesus appeared, and God's Spirit was abroad in the world before its superabundant release in Jesus' death/resurrection. Both Word and Spirit, therefore, have broader scope than their tie to Jesus, even if he was their all-time fullest and most definitive manifestation. Thus people of other times and cultures can have genuine contact with God, be within the ambience of God's Word and Spirit, and experience God's salvation without knowing Jesus or hearing his particular teachings.

Karl Rahner is well known for his theology of implicit or anonymous Christianity. It is derived from the same two basic notions as his Christology: the human person as the mystery of infinite emptiness and God as the mystery of infinite fullness. God is the horizon in the life of every person, experienced at the edge of consciousness. God reaches out graciously to every person, and is at least dimly known by every person as that mysterious power in human life that both challenges and comforts. Whenever anyone opens to that mystery and responds to it in attitudes and choices, that person displays faith, even if he or she does not acknowledge God or Christ by name. By what signs can we know that someone has this implicit faith? It shows itself in hope and love. Those who have it are hopeful even in the midst of adversity. They believe that life is worth living, that it still makes sense to move forward into tomorrow, that things will somehow work out. And in some measure at least they love. They apply themselves to their daily responsibilities, take care of their families, transcend selfishness in their relationships with at least some people in their world. By these manifestations of hope and love, we know the presence of their implicit faith or yes-saying to God.

The genuine atheist is not someone who says, "I do not believe in God." It is someone who has never given or accepted love and who cares absolutely nothing for justice or truth. Such persons are rare. In the vast majority of human lives, we find hope and love, at least in some measure. In Jesus of Nazareth we find them most fully, because his was the fullest yes to God. Even in our lives as *explicit* Christians, the call is no greater than to live out our faith as fully as possible in hope and love. Any Scripture passage we read at the liturgy or use for personal prayer will be exhorting us either to the one or to the other. God's program for implicit and explicit Christians is the same. But explicit Christians have many advantages in living this vocation precisely because their faith is explicit, its supports tangible.

Rahner's name of "anonymous Christian" or "implicit Christian" for those persons who respond to God's gracious outreach in their lives without an explicit Christian commitment has come under criticism. It does not appeal to those who are so named, any more than it would appeal to a Christian to be called an "anonymous Buddhist." Most of us prefer to have our self-descriptions taken seriously. We feel fairly sure that we know what we are, and being told that we are really something else without knowing it cannot but sound patronizing.

But the difficulty may be deeper than diplomacy. Rahner is persuaded that there is only one mediator, Jesus Christ, and that all grace comes through him. Thus, even though there is no empirical evidence that those whose lives exhibit hope and love are under the influence of Jesus, Rahner holds that they are. Other theologians see it a little differently. Not everything that comes from God has to come through Jesus, because the reality of God is not exhausted in the reality of Jesus. Jesus is an *historical* reality. There is a Scripture, a teaching, a life, an institution in which his influence is embodied. Some people come within this ambience and open to it. Others do not. There is no real justification for calling the latter Christians, and no need to. For God's relationship to the world through Word and Spirit is larger than the incarnation in Jesus of Nazareth. Process theologians keep us reminded of this point in their treatment of the logos (or God's Word), but its grounds are in the New Testament itself, as we saw in our consideration of Jesus' pre-existence. There have been other historical persons in whom God's Word has been eloquently spoken, other scriptures in which the Spirit of God has been at work, and other historical institutions which embody these influences. Besides these, there is the depth of every human heart, that private, silent region which is plumbed by the Spirit of God. Jesus is but one avenue to and from God, even if he is the principal one.

IMPLICATIONS FOR CHRISTIAN MINISTRY

If we accept the latter, broader view of God's universal salvific will and activity on behalf of all human beings, there are important ramifications for Christian missionary activity, Christian evangelization, and our dialogue with the other religions and with atheism.

Would it still make sense to send out missionaries to countries which are predominantly non-Christian? Yes, but the understanding of this activity and the purpose envisioned would be different than they have usually been. The motive would no longer be to snatch souls from hell by baptism. Nor would it be to rescue people from "pagan superstitions" by Christian teaching. It would not even be primarily to make converts to the Christian religion, though converts would certainly be welcome. The purpose of Christian mission would be simply to share the good news and to live the Christian life among and for other people. Good news cries out to be shared, even if there is little danger that people will end in hell if they do not fully accept it. Christians are enthusiasts, people who have found a treasure buried in a field, and we spontaneously want others to enjoy the same good thing. So we talk about it, and offer the same free opportunity to others. Besides that, Christian people are servants, in the spirit of Jesus. We go to places where we see other people in need, need of any kind, and minister to that need. Thus Christian mission will always be valid and important.

Evangelization is a variation of mission. It too is the sharing of the good news. It too is outreach in the Christian spirit to those in any kind of need. And it continues to make sense for the same reasons.

Whether it be mission abroad or evangelization at home, what should be one's attitude if people do not respond by joining the Church? Has one failed? Have these people been unaffected? Most likely the people have been affected in some way. They may have been moved to be better Hindus, Jews, Buddhists, or "atheists," by the influence of genuinely good Christians. The leaven is in the mass, and it is working there even if many of its effects escape observation. For that matter, the Christians in the encounter have probably also been moved to be better Christians by the influence of genuinely good Hindus, Buddhists, Jews, or "atheists." At least that is usually how it works.

Karl Rahner has a couple of interesting reflections on atheists which fit in at this point. It is not as obvious as it might seem just what atheists are rejecting. It may not be God at all. It may be the inauthentic ways they see Christians and other religious people living. They find that unattractive. It may be the theological presentation of God they have been exposed to; they find *that* impossible to believe. Neither of these rejections is at all the same as rejecting God, to whom they may be responding within themselves. That is why Rahner runs the test on their lives rather than on their utterances. Rahner's final point is that if we want to understand that rare breed of person we call an atheist, we might begin with the atheist who lurks in the breast of each of us believers. Very few of us are free of tendencies toward unbelief.

What should be the Christian attitude in dialoguing with members of other religions? In the past it has so often been an attitude of arrogance:

> "We are going to heaven, but you are going to hell."
> "We have the true religion; your religion is the work of Satan."
> "The founder of our religion is God; your founder was a mere human being."
> "We believe we are in contact with God, and we are right; you believe you are in contact with God, but you are quite wrong."

To any fair-minded person hearing this "dialogue" and looking at the lives of the parties involved, these remarks would be unmistakably arrogant and certainly not manifestly true. They derive from unexamined assumptions, and scarcely have a place in the modern world of religious diversity. The Christian attitude in the dialogue with the religions should rather be one of respect and reverence. We have much to learn, much to be enriched by, not only in other religious ideas but probably even more in other religious persons. It is always healthy to have one's horizons of understanding expanded, and to bring more diverse elements into one's worldview. The American Protestant theologian Wilfred Cantwell Smith beautifully displays this attitude in his writings on comparative religion. Surely this would be the spirit of Jesus were he alive for the dialogue of the religions today. It was his spirit even two thousand years ago, when he found and endorsed the good in all the unlikeliest places and saw plenty of evil in the religious institutions sanctioned by his culture.

The Second Vatican Council expresses a positive attitude toward the non-Christian religions, accepting them as ways of salvation, and encouraging Christian dialogue with them. It also affirms the possibility of salvation for professed atheists who sincerely seek the truth and try to do what is right as they understand it.

Before we leave this matter of the interaction between Christians and adherents of other religions, we might note the many benefits that have come to us through this contact in recent years. We have been able to incorporate many of the attitudes and practices of Eastern and Sufi mysticism into our own prayer, and find ourselves enriched. This has led to a renewed interest in our Western mystical tradition and prompted us to make it available to more of our own people. We have learned yoga, and found it beneficial for body and mind, and a fine preparation for contemplation. Our contact with Mohandas Gandhi and his non-violent approach to social and political change has gotten us back in touch with the non-violence in our own Gospels, and shown us how to put it into action. Impressed with these gifts from other religious traditions, the well-known American Trappist monk Thomas Merton wrote more and more in his later years on the positive contributions of the Eastern religions. Merton was attending an international congress on mysticism in Bangkok when he died.

In a world of religious diversity, respectful dialogue and collaboration are the only sensible attitudes. Religious exclusivism is a dubious course in any case. It comes more from the human desire to be righteous and to have a boast over others than it does from a real grasp of the truth, which particularly in religious matters is always beyond us all.

QUESTIONS FOR DISCUSSION

1. What are some of the considerations which make us question whether being a Christian is the only way to be saved?
2. Can one take the New Testament seriously and at the same time hold that a person can be saved without faith in Christ and baptism?
3. What is Rahner's theology of implicit or anonymous Christianity? Do you agree with it?
4. Among the many theologies presented here of Jesus' role in human salvation, which is closest to your own position?
5. If Christian faith and baptism are not absolutely necessary for salvation, what are the implications for Christian mission, evangelization, and the dialogue with non-Christian religions?

Afterword

There is an alternate version of the Caesarea Philippi incident which did not make it into the New Testament canon.

> Jesus came with his disciples one day to Caesarea Philippi, and he said to them: "Who do people say I am?" And they said to him: "You are the Revealer." "You are the absolute, unsurpassable victory of God's self-bestowal." "You are the second person of the Blessed Trinity." "You are unbroken contact with the Ground of Being." "You are the Man for Others." "You are the Word incarnate." "You are the proleptic manifestation of the eschaton."
>
> And Jesus said, "What?"

Efforts to interpret Jesus never end. Sometimes they become so complex that even Jesus is not sure what they mean. The final test of any Christology is not as much theoretical as it is practical: the kind of life it gives rise to. "By their fruits you shall know them," Jesus said, addressing the question of true and false prophets (Mt 7:20). The test is a good one for a theological interpretation of Jesus. Does it elicit genuine discipleship? Does it make God's salvation in Jesus available with maximal power to the world?

Christian discipleship and the power of the good news to save have perhaps never been as important as they are at the present time. As we face the immense economic imbalance of our world and the threat of total destruction by nuclear war, we stand in critical need of vision, energy, a program of action, and hope.

146

Our Christian faith offers us all four. The vision is that of the goal of human history, the coming together of humankind into one body, a body we call Christ. The only possible energy for that is charity. The program of action is seen in the ministry of Jesus: an unshakable faith in the goodness of every person, respect and a desire for dialogue, non-violence even in the face of violence, a willingness to sacrifice what one has for the benefit of others. The basis of our hope is the love with which God embraces our fragile world and cherishes our human project, and God's presence and power in our midst.

It was insights such as these that prompted the Roman Catholic priest and scientist Pierre Teilhard de Chardin to reformulate Christology for the tasks of the twentieth century. He appreciated the peculiar gifts of vision, energy, tactics, and hope that come to us from Jesus, and saw the imperious need for them at this critical juncture of history. More than anywhere else, it was on the community of Christians that he placed the burden of responsibility for the direction that evolution takes from here. Are we willing to shoulder that burden and continue the struggle to bring in the reign of God?

Suggestions for Further Reading

The following works figure in varying degrees into the synthesis of this book. The list is by no means exhaustive of worthwhile works on Christology.

D.M. Baillie	**God Was in Christ,** Scribner's, 1948
L. Boff	**Jesus Christ Liberator,** Orbis, 1978
D. Bonhoeffer	**Christ the Center,** Harper, 1966
———	**Letters and Papers from Prison,** Macmillan, 1967
G. Bornkamm	**Jesus of Nazareth,** Harper, 1960
R. Brown	**Jesus God and Man,** Bruce, 1967
———	**The Virginal Conception and Bodily Resurrection of Jesus,** Paulist, 1973
R. Bultmann	**Theology of the New Testament,** Scribner's, 1951
J. Cobb	**Christ in a Pluralistic Age,** Westminster, 1975
J. Cobb and D. Griffin	**Process Theology,** Westminster 1976
M. Cook	**The Jesus of Faith,** Paulist, 1982
A. Dulles	**The Survival of Dogma,** Doubleday, 1971

J. Dwyer	**Son of Man and Son of God,** Paulist, 1983
J. Fitzmyer	**A Christological Catechism,** Paulist, 1982
G. Gutierrez	**A Theology of Liberation,** Orbis, 1973
W. Kasper	**Jesus the Christ,** Paulist, 1976
J. Knox	**The Humanity and Divinity of Christ,** Cambridge, 1967
H. Kung	**On Being a Christian,** Doubleday, 1966
D. Lane	**The Reality of Jesus,** Paulist, 1975
S. Marrow	**The Words of Jesus in Our Gospels: A Catholic Response to Fundamentalism,** Paulist, 1982
J. Moltmann	**The Crucified God,** Harper, 1974
C. Mooney	**Teilhard de Chardin and the Mystery of Christ,** Doubleday, 1968
S. Moore	**The Fire and the Rose Are One,** Seabury, 1980
————	**The Crucified Jesus Is No Stranger,** Seabury, 1981
J. O'Grady	**Models of Jesus,** Doubleday, 1982
W. Pannenberg	**Jesus God and Man,** Westminster, 1968

N. Pittenger   **The Word Incarnate,**Harper,
                             1959

————   **Catholic Faith in a Process
                             Perspective,** Orbis, 1981

K. Rahner   **Theological Investigations,** passim
                             Seabury

————   **Foundations of Christian Faith,**
                             Seabury, 1978

E. Schillebeeckx   **Jesus,** Seabury, 1979

————   **Jesus and Christ,** Crossroad, 1981

————   **Christ,** Crossroad, 1981

P. Schineller   "Christ and Church: A Spectrum of
                             Views" **Theological Studies,**
                             December 1976

P. Schoonenberg   **The Christ,** Herder, 1971

————   " 'He Emptied Himself':
                             Philippians 2:7" in **Concilium,** XI,
                             Paulist,   1956

W.C. Smith   **The Meaning and End of Religion,**
                             New American Library, 1964

————   **Religious Diversity,** Crossroad,
                             1982

P. Smulders   **The Fathers on Christology** St.
                             Norbert's Abbey Press, 1968

J. Sobrino   **Christology at the Crossroads,**
                             Orbis, 1978

P. Teilhard de Chardin	**The Divine Milieu,** Harper, 1960
————	**The Future of Man,** Harper, 1969
————	**Hymn of the Universe,** Harper, 1965
P. Tillich	**Systematic Theology,** University of Chicago, 1967
————	**Christianity and the Encounter of the World Religions,** Columbia Univ., 1963
A. Toynbee	**Christianity Among the Religions of the World,** Scribner's, 1957
G. van der Leeuw	**Religion in Essence and Manifestation,** (2 vols) Harper, 1963
J. Wallace	**The Call to Conversion,** Harper, 1981
A.N. Whitehead	**Adventures of Ideas,** Free Press, 1967
————	**Process and Reality,** Free Press, 1969
————	**Religion in the Making,** Meridian, 1960